An Integrative
Approach to
Managing Innovation

An Integrative Approach to Managing Innovation

Judith Brown Kamm
Bentley College

Lexington Books
D.C. Heath and Company/Lexington, Massachusetts/Toronto

Library of Congress Cataloging-in-Publication Data

Kamm, Judith Brown.
  An integrative approach to managing innovation.

  Includes index.
  1. Technological innovations. I. Title.
T173.8.K35 1987   658.4'063   85-45798
ISBN 0-669-12339-0 (alk. paper)

Copyright © 1987 by D.C. Heath and Company

Published simultaneously in Canada
Printed in the United States of America
Casebound International Standard Book Number: 0-669-12339-0
Library of Congress Catalog Card Number 85-45798

The paper used in this publication meets the minimum requirements of
American National Standard for Information Sciences—Permanence of
Paper for Printed Library Materials, ANSI Z39.48-1984. ∞™

87 88 89 90 91 8 7 6 5 4 3 2 1

For Roger, Meredith, and Peter,
who managed my innovation.

Contents

Figures and Tables

Figures

Tables

Acknowledgments

Many people have helped this book to become a reality. I am especially grateful to the anonymous managers who have been most generous with their time and experience in providing the field data for my research. Thanks, also, to Doug Bailey, Steve Ardussi, Vicki Carr, Larry Young, and Denise Gagnon Leeco for helping me to target my audience in presenting the findings and my ideas.

Without the wisdom of Jay Lorsch, Bill Bruns, and Steve Palesy and funding from Harvard Business School's Division of Research, my project never would have been feasible. Hans Pennings and several anonymous reviewers contributed much to the evolution of my thinking. I am in their debt.

My colleagues at Bentley College have also assisted me. I am particularly appreciative of Aaron Nurick's collaboration in our research project on small, young companies. Tony Buono's ideas on corporate social responsiveness have given me a new perspective on innovation. My Mg652: *Management of Innovation* (Spring 1986) class was also helpful in providing feedback and suggestions. The management department's secretarial staff has supported me with amazing good nature, especially Jessica Liles, who typed the nastiest parts of the manuscript (the tables). Thanks, too, go to Don Brown, Bentley's graphics producer, who helped me make visual sense of my ideas.

Bruce Katz, my editor, has shown humor and patience as I've brought my work to completion. Thank you, one and all.

Introduction

I n the past twenty years, countless articles and books have been written on the topic of managing innovation. In much of this work, it has become conventional to define the problem as organizations' insufficient or failed innovation. Typically, the blame for failures to innovate successfully or at all is placed upon management, if not directly, then by implication. Managers are then exhorted to be more innovative or to stop stifling other people's creativity: methods are prescribed for increasing innovation and improving its success rate. Managers, in turn, often blame academics for offering impractical advice.

Consequently, despite the amount of attention that both scholars and practitioners have paid to improving the management of innovation, the flood of printed material continues unabated. Innovations are attempted and fail. And, in a recent *Management Science* article entitled "Central Problems in the Management of Innovation" (May 1986, pp. 590–607), Andrew Van de Ven reported that many chief executive officers of large companies view innovation as their most vital concern for this decade. He notes that very little work, however, has been done to address this concern from general management's point of view.

It appears that many of us keep pushing the same old buttons to solve the problem of innovation, but the problem is not being solved. Perhaps we are making some unrealistic assumptions about it. This book questions many of them, such as the assumptions that innovation is always good; the more radical it is, the better; the most successful organizations are always the most innovative; and tight managerial control stifles innovation.

Such questioning leads to a different definition of the central problem in managing innovation. Instead of trying to solve the problem of how organizations can innovate more and better, this book addresses the issue of how to make better decisions about innovation. That is, how can organizations innovate more selectively and wisely so that their objectives are achieved?

Note that the word *wisely* rather than *rationally* is used here. One of the same old buttons that we keep pressing to improve the management of innovation seems to be to make the innovation process and our decisions about it as rational as possible. Wisdom comes from intuition and emotion as well as from intellect and rational analysis. Innovation is not a rational phenomenon. No matter how much we may try to rationalize it, we will fail. We stand a better chance of managing it successfully if we accept this reality and find other ways of working with it.

Furthermore, innovation is rarely undertaken for its own sake, for the pure and simple pleasure of it. The reason for this should be obvious to anyone who has ever tried to do anything new. The process is rarely, if ever, purely pleasurable. In fact, it can be costly and painful. Thus, there is usually some deeper need or more long-term objective that a person or an organization's management is trying to satisfy or achieve by innovating. These needs and objectives vary widely among individuals and organizations, yet, if they are met, success results, at least for that person or organization.

Innovation may not always be the best way to achieve a particular goal, however. It is not assumed here to be a panacea. For example, an organization wanting to consolidate and regain stability after a period of rapid, chaotic growth may not be successful in doing so if it innovates during this period. Therefore, a successful decision about an innovation proposal may be to reject it, to postpone consideration of it until later, or to consider it for implementation some time in the future.

Good decision making in general, and especially about innovation, is based upon two essential processes. One process is analysis, or breaking down the subject into its elemental parts. The other process is integration, or pulling together these elements—either with each other or with unrelated parts—in such a way that a greater understanding of the original subject is achieved.

This book analyzes innovation by breaking it down into the pieces most relevant to general managers. The different types of innovation, the phases it passes through, and the issues and problems of controlling it during each of these phases are laid out for examination. The main emphasis is on integration, however, as the title indicates.

One reason for this emphasis is the belief, shared by at least one other author in this field, Rosabeth Moss Kanter, that innovation is too often based solely upon rational analysis and "segmentalist" problem solving and organizational design. Such an approach taken by itself is inadequate for successful innovation. Emphasizing integration in this book, then, is an attempt to balance our strong natural tendency to take things apart and then to leave them for someone else to put back together again.

Another reason for taking an integrative approach to the problem of managing innovation is that it is most appropriate for the general managers to whom this book is addressed. Middle- and top-level managers in most organizations must be generalists who can pull together information from a wide variety of sources because they are responsible for more than one organizational unit and/or function. Their comprehensive responsibilities dictate that they have a broader understanding of their organization, including the differing interests, goals, styles, and capabilities of people in the units that comprise it.

General managers must also be able to discern the similarities underlying these differences so that they can set a direction that all parts can achieve and so that they can coordinate them so that they do not thwart each other in following it. Thus, part of the job of the general manager is to think integratively and to act as an integrator, or one who brings together disparate elements into a coherent whole. Pulling together the disparate pieces of anything requires that there be some underlying unity or set of similarities across all the pieces.

This approach to innovation is integrated by focussing upon its essential nature. The similarities among all forms of innovation are then used as determinants of the book's structure and contents. All innovation is assumed to be a process of events occurring over time. Therefore, this book's organization follows the most common sequence of phases through which general managers follow an idea for any kind of innovation. As figure I-1 indicates, these phases include formulating innovation strategies, generating and testing ideas, selling ideas in order to get resources, selecting innovations, implementing them, and relating the entire process to the organization's environment.

The innovation process is portrayed as circular, with double-headed arrows between its phases to represent the idea that as new things evolve, they often

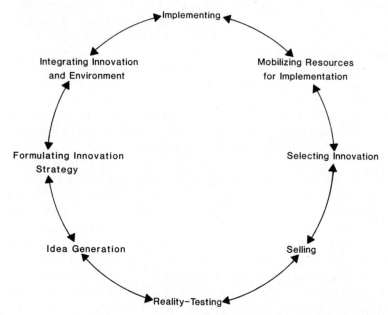

Figure I-1. An Integrative Approach to Organizational Innovation

stop and return to an earlier phase. Later phases can affect earlier ones, and vice versa. Previously completed innovations' impact upon the organization's environment can be a factor in formulating current and future innovation strategies. This integrative approach to innovation, then, does not view it as a linear phenomenon, despite the fact that the sequencing of the chapters may make it appear that way.

Another similarity among all forms of innovation is that they are special cases of human behavior. As a new idea evolves, decisions about it are generally made at increasingly higher authority levels of the organization. Conflicts in goals, values, attitudes, and behavioral styles may occur in this process. Thus, innovation can be very much influenced by relationships between individuals and between groups or departments. Resolving the inevitable conflicts is essential if the innovation is to occur. Innovation, then, is a political process that requires interpersonal skills for successful management. Consequently, applied behavioral science concepts from the literature on leadership, organizational development, and power and politics are used throughout this book.

Behavioral science, however, is not the only knowledge area tapped as a source of ideas to apply to the management of innovation. Just as innovation is a multifunctional activity in most companies because it requires a variety of departments in order to be brought to fruition, so, too, is an integrative approach to managing it interdisciplinary. Among the other business disciplines drawn from to prepare this book are: business policy (formulating and implementing strategy), marketing (new-product development, market research, and sales), production and operations management (adopting new technology), entrepreneurship (creating new markets and organizations), and corporate financial management (allocating resources for innovation).

Finally, this book is integrative in that it combines descriptions of managerial practice found in field-based study as well as in the business press with prescriptions based upon common sense and theoretical literature. These prescriptions take the form of issues for general managers to consider plus conceptual frameworks for making sense of experience.

The research upon which some of this book is based began with a pilot study of the impact of a wide range of new-product development procedures upon individual creativity and risk taking in six consumer goods divisions of large companies in a wide variety of industries, from amateur photography to beverages. The data gathering consisted of preliminary examination of annual reports, 10K and proxy statements, and other publicly available information, followed by interviews with the division general manager or equivalent, a new-product manager or equivalent, and any other relevant new-product developers.

The next phase of the project was to examine the impact of selected administrative control systems on the innovative behavior of scientists and engineers in three integrated circuit semiconductor divisions and four ethical pharmaceuticals divisions of seven large firms. These firms all had the following characteristics: annual corporate sales of at least $25 million, annual corporate R&D expenditures of at least $1 million, public ownership, nonfamily management, and primary reliance upon internally developed new products. In order to place each division's control systems in the proper context, data about its strategy were gathered in interviews with general managers. The control systems were also described by the managers who in some cases had designed them and in all cases were responsible for implementing them.

Almost 400 questionnaires were distributed to engineers and scientists, and 218 were returned by mail. Background information about the individual new-product developers was gathered in addition to their perceptions and attitudes about the way in which their innovation activities were managed. Their innovative behavior itself was measured in a variety of ways using self-reported data. When the questionnaires had been received and the quantitative data from them had been organized into some meaningful display, a research case was written about each of the seven divisions.

In addition to this study, an ongoing research project on informal social systems in small, young software companies is a source of examples. These firms are full of innovation. New organizations are adopting new processes to make or market new products in a new industry. A panel of general managers from such diverse organizations as an architectural design firm, a major bank, and a bedding company has also contributed ideas and observations about their own experience to the preparation of this manuscript.

Many of the ideas in this book have been tested and refined by using them in Bentley College's M.B.A. course on managing innovation. In it, practicing and prospective managers from such different industries as health care, financial services, and computer manufacturing shared their experiences, frustrations, and ideas on this subject.

Thus, over the past eight years, the disparate material for this book has accumulated and a variety of connections have been made. The very creation of the following chapters has involved using an integrative approach to innovating. Experiencing the very phenomenon that one is writing about has lent insights that would not have been possible otherwise. While much work remains to be done in this area, it is hoped that the approach taken here will be a useful step in the right direction.

An Integrative
Approach to
Managing Innovation

1

Key Innovation Decisions

Managers make decisions about many different kinds of innovation as an important part of their jobs. For instance, the director of the architectural design unit of a large design services company had to decide about adopting and updating computer-assisted design equipment for the first time in his firm. He was also involved in devising a unique series of interdepartmental committees to make other important companywide decisions. Similarly, the manufacturing vice president of a company in the bedding industry approved and implemented not only the adoption of the most modern European quilting equipment, but also the computerization of all inventory for better administrative control.

Although these activities appear to have little in common, because they are forms of innovation, they have two unifying factors: (1) the nature of innovation itself and (2) the conditions and effects commonly associated with innovation. The following analysis of these commonalities should provide a better understanding of innovation in general, an important foundation for making decisions about it.

Innovation Defined

Innovation is the process of generating ideas new to their source and making decisions about these ideas, resulting in something useful. The first term in this definition that deserves elaboration is *process*. The integrative approach views innovation as a series of events that comes into being and that changes over time. All forms of innovation are believed to occur in phases, some of which may be repeated or skipped. In this respect, the integrative approach is similar to most other ways of thinking about innovation.[1]

No attempt is made here, however, to discover the attributes of a particular innovation (outcome) and its surrounding conditions in static terms in order to explain why it came to be and why it is having whatever effects it has. Furthermore, the integrative approach does not view innovation as an organizational quality to be understood in order to be attained or enhanced.[2]

Instead, that which precedes innovation and what happens during the process are examined in order to understand it. The ultimate purpose of this analysis is to permit decision makers to better decide whether and under what constraints to allow or encourage it to happen.

The next key term is *decisions*. Regardless of the form that innovation takes, at each step of the process, general managers must make a set of decisions. To formulate innovation strategy the following questions must be answered: What problems or opportunities currently exist that would best be handled by doing something new? What objectives would be achieved by innovating? How much innovation can the organization support in the short- and long-term? What type of innovation is needed, given the demand for it and the organizational and environmental context within which it should occur?

To manage the idea phase of innovation, decisions need to be made about what resources will stimulate new ideas and whether or not they are available. Managers must also decide how long they can wait for ideas to bubble up from lower levels of the organization and whether there are any individuals whose ideas should be especially sought out and encouraged. To oversee the reality-testing of new ideas that are generated, managers should ask, how much strategic information should we provide to help innovators assess their ideas' feasibility? Also, how formal and extensive should we require the data-gathering procedures to be to serve as the basis for subsequent proposals?

At the proposal or selling phase of any kind of innovation, general management decides how many and what kinds of requirements there should be for proposals submitted for its review. Other questions to answer could include how much informal preselling do we require or tolerate from innovators and how open should we be about what our selection criteria are so that proposers can better target their pitches to us?

In their most important role as the judges of which innovations will be approved for completion, top-level managers must decide upon the criteria that have to be met in order for resources to be allocated to innovation proposals. Another question is how much they should intervene in suggesting improvements in proposals for resubmission. Are these either/or or yes/no choices, or do they negotiate with proposers in terms of amount of resources, scope of undertaking, time frames, and so on?

When implementing the innovations that have been selected, managers must decide how to establish budgets for them, whom to put in charge of insuring that they are executed as promised in proposals, how to gain the acceptance and commitment of the rest of the organization, whether or not to reserve the right to change its mind and stop the innovation process if promises are not kept, and how to present the completed innovation to the company's internal and external stakeholders.

The term *new* requires further elaboration because it is quite ambiguous. Perhaps its only universally accepted meaning is that it is something different in some way from what preceded it. The difference may only be in the eyes of the beholder, or it may be widely acknowledged as different. It may not resemble anything existing previously or it may resemble something closely. It may differ in a variety of ways or in only one way. The quality of newness itself, then, can be described along three dimensions: (1) the judge's view (ranging from unique to widely shared), (2) the degree of similarity to existing things in its class or its starting a new class, and (3) the scope of ways in which it is similar to existing things. All of these dimensions occur along a continuum.

The term *useful* is also important in the integrative definition of innovation. Marketing experts are particularly emphatic about the need to include this in any conception of innovation.[3] Like the term *new*, this part of the definition requires elaboration because it, too, is ambiguous. The extent to which an idea is useful depends upon the attitudes of the person or persons ascribing these characteristics. No attempt is made here to give objective criteria for making such determinations. Utility, too, is a matter of degree.

The Dimensions of Innovation

Investigators of innovation have attempted to identify and characterize types of innovation as a natural part of their research. General managers need to be able to identify the type of innovation they are making decisions about because some types make different demands upon the organization than do others. In fact, identification should precede decision making.

Most existing taxonomies of innovation are limited to one or two dimensions. For example, the degree of newness is frequently used and has been subdivided into two rough categories: variation or evolution; and reorientation or revolution.[4] Another common dimension is the source of the newness, such as the organization,[5] the market, the technology, or the product or the process.[6] These dimensions are then commonly juxtaposed as in Edgar Pessemier's well-known taxonomy, which produces nine types of product innovation objectives, ranging from reformulation to diversification.[7]

Two other common dimensions, which are frequently confused with each other, are timing of market entry and competitive posture.[8] Timing of market entry has usually been subdivided into the categories of first-to-the-market, rapid second or third, and late.[9] In the innovation adoption or diffusion literature, analogous categories are innovators, early adopters, early majority, late majority, and laggards.[10]

Competitive postures are commonly described as pioneering, adaptive, and imitative[11] or market segmentation.[12] Yet another dimension is traits contributing to diffusion. The categories of this dimension are: relative advantage, compatibility, complexity (difficulty of user comprehension), divisibility (ability to offer samples for trial use), and communicability (ability to display for user observation).[13]

In addition to being limited to two dimensions, which necessarily excludes the others mentioned here, existing taxonomies of innovation reflect the relatively crude forms of measurement that have been used along each dimension. By nature, some of them, such as source of innovation or competitive posture, are categorical, that is, not amenable to mathematical manipulation. In other words, they cannot be added together to produce any meaningful result. Other dimensions, however, such as degree of newness, are more continuous, as the word *degree* implies. Unfortunately, this dimension has been treated more like a categorical variable having two values, revolutionary and evolutionary, to represent extremely new things and not-so-new things, respectively.

There is need for a more comprehensive categorization scheme for innovation that integrates and consolidates, yet clearly distinguishes among, the dimensions previously mentioned here in order for decision makers to more accurately understand what kind of innovation they are considering. Furthermore, in specifying these dimensions, researchers need finer, more precise distinctions in the scales measuring them.

Table 1–1 not only presents a synthesis of previous work in this area, but also suggests an improvement upon it by making clearer distinctions among dimensions and making the measurement scales more precise. Discussions of each of the four dimensions follow.

Form

This dimension is the most basic in its description of what is new. Is it a product, process, service, organizational structure, or organizational procedure? Are the decision makers viewing it as something generated for others' use or as something adopted for their own or their organization's use?

The new thing occurs in one of the three fundamental components of any organization's existence: its technology (defined as "any tool or technique, any physical equipment or method of doing or making, by which human capability is extended"[14]), its market (the aggregate of its users, buyers, or clients), and its own organization (structure and function).

Another way of thinking about the form of innovation is in terms of its originating location. For instance, is it a market or market segment that is being entered for the first time (market adoption)? Is it a manufacturing process that has never been used before (technology adoption)? Is it an in-house–developed method for supervising employees that has never before been used (generation of organizational procedure)? While these variations in the form of innovation are often related to each other (process and product are commonly considered

Table 1–1
Types of Innovation: A Classification Scheme

Form:
> Generation or adoption of technological product, process, or service
> Generation or adoption of market
> Generation or adoption of organizational structure or procedure

Function:
> Improves quality
> Reduces cost
> Performs functions not previously performed
> Enhances attractiveness for current market
> Increases offerings to current market
> Enters market not currently served
> Improves learning curve (unit cost decreases as experience increases)
> Enhances economies of scale
> Permits production of better-quality offering
> Enhances human growth and potential

Extent:
> From 0° (no difference from reference point) to 180° (new reference point)

Timing:
> First-to-market (or first-to-adopt)
> Quick second
> Quick third
> Late follower

a unit[15]), they are different enough to be singled out as a first stage in categorizing any particular innovation.

Function

In this book, *innovation* is defined as "the process of generating ideas new to their source and making decisions about these ideas, resulting in something useful." The function of a particular innovation, then, is that which makes it useful. What purpose does the innovation serve? Another way of thinking about this dimension is to view it as the objective of the innovation. Pessemier and Philip Marvin have categorized the types of functions performed by new products, and Michael Porter has categorized those performed by new processes.[16] These have been integrated into the first nine of the ten functions listed in table 1–1.

The tenth function, "enhances human growth and development," is an original addition. It means that some innovations are not specifically developed for commercial purposes. They may be commercialized ultimately, as Polaroid did with its in-house personnel training program, but their conception is aimed at a broader purpose. "Growth and development" means advancement in human skills and capabilities, including intellectual ones (information processing, decision making, and understanding), physical ones (strength, dexterity, and endurance), and emotional ones (sensitivity and control).

Extent

This dimension is probably the one most commonly used to identify and categorize innovation. It includes consideration of whether something new is an adaptation (making significant changes in) or imitation (making insignificant changes in) of that which exists. The question that it answers is, "How new is this new thing?" Although something can be new in a variety of ways, and a complete answer can only be derived from identifying it along each of the four dimensions listed in table 1–1, it is possible to distinguish a separate dimension for this attribute.

Unlike the form and function dimensions, which are categorical or nominal variables, this dimension is a matter of degree of difference from a reference point. Thus, it is an ordinal variable. In other words, something new is more or less different from its closest genotype (or class of objects or ideas) as defined by their form and function.

One way of conceptualizing degree of newness is to consider the new thing as a central point in a semicircle ranging from 0 degrees (exact identity with that which already exists) to 180 degrees (complete difference from that which already exists, thus creating a new class). An arrow could be drawn from the central point representing the innovation to the degree on the arc best indicating how new the innovation is, as is shown in figure 1–1. While this form of measurement is arbitrary, and the actual determination of which degree of newness any given innovation achieves may be subjective, it does capture the nature of the phenomenon. It also permits at least some quantitative measurement of it.

Some innovations can be quite complex, making it difficult to gauge just how new they are. One approach is to break down the new thing into its major parts in order to locate and determine the newness of the innovation. A ratio of new parts to old parts, also known as compatibility,[17] expressed as a percentage, could be determined, which could then be applied to the original scale of 0–180 degrees.

For example, a computer could be considered an innovation if it had a larger-capacity memory than any other computer in its class. If this memory was its only new component, and if this component comprised 20 percent of its major parts, then the computer itself would be categorized as having 36 degrees of newness ($.20 \times 180$). It would be "compatible" rather than "discontinuous."[18]

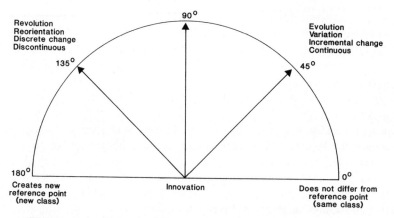

Figure 1–1. Extent of Innovation: "How New Is New?"

While the memory device alone might be a breakthrough, having much closer to 180 degrees of newness, if the entire computer were being considered, then the other parts would be considered as well.

This example highlights the importance of carefully and explicitly defining the boundaries of the innovation being categorized. In decision making about whether to continue developing or to adopt something new, such detailed analysis is a step toward better management of uncertainty. In other words, having a clear idea about how much of something is very new (and therefore uncertain) can prevent misperceptions about risk of failure or loss that can inhibit innovation.

Timing

The timing or precedence of an innovation is another dimension that should be included in any complete description of it.[19] The timing of an innovation is its availability on a market or adoption by a user relative to its first introduction or use anywhere. Traditionally, there have been three rough categories of timing applied to new products or services: first-to-the-market, also known as pioneering or leading; quick second or third; and late follower. Comparable categories have been used to describe adopting users.

When an innovation appears can importantly affect how new it is perceived to be, regardless of its objective degree of newness. The earlier or sooner something is offered to a market, a market is opened, or something is used, the greater the uncertainty about its performance and its impact in general. There may be little experience accumulated about the innovation; thus, trial-and-error learning—the most expensive kind—occurs. On the other hand, if this experience is kept proprietary, it can become a benefit instead of a cost. Ability to set prices, quality standards, and other parameters of the innovation to benefit the leading generator or adopter can also be significant advantages offsetting the problems associated with being the first.

Being the second or third to appear does not necessarily mean that the innovation is exactly like the first to the market. Nor does being first to the market necessarily mean that the innovation has a high degree of newness. It is possible to be the first with a slight variation in a revolutionary innovation; this has been called "leapfrogging."[20]

Using the Classification Scheme

Because innovation is such a relative, perceptual phenomenon, the first step in using the classification scheme in table 1–1 is to select a point of view. In this integrative approach to innovation (which is designed to improve decision making about innovation in general), the decision makers' point of view (or that of their organization) is taken. Thus, if the decision makers' organization is generating or adopting something for the first time, it is innovation, regardless of what other organizations have or have not done about it.

As mentioned previously, the second step in classifying the innovation is to put boundaries on it. How much of it, if it is part of a system or package, is to be classified? In order to fully describe the innovation as it has been delimited, information about each of the four dimensions must be obtained. It does not matter which dimension is considered first, although there may be some intuitive appeal in moving from top to bottom in table 1–1. On the first two dimensions, form and function of innovation, any given new thing may fall into more than one subgroup. For example, a hybrid technology-market innovation may serve several purposes, such as improving quality and making the product more attractive for the current market.

On the other hand, any given innovation cannot be both radically new, with, say, 140 degrees of difference from what currently exists, and not so new, with, say, 50 degrees of difference at the same time. Similarly, any given innovation cannot both be a pioneer and a late follower at the same time.

For example, a radically new chemical compound for the treatment of arthritis can only be radically new for the purpose for which it is intended (helping arthritis) by the organization developing it. Furthermore, in the form presently being categorized, it cannot simultaneously be introduced first and later to the same market of physicians treating human arthritis patients. However, if the same compound were to be introduced to a very different market (such as veterinarians), then a different innovation would present itself for categorization.

The Behavioral Nature of Innovation

No matter how it is defined or categorized, innovation is a peculiarly human phenomenon. Innovation begins in the human mind, whether it is the concept or invention from which new products, services, and systems result,[21] or the awareness of the existence of something new from which adoption and diffusion result.[22] Just as innovation cannot be easily separated from the people who make it happen, so behavior cannot be easily separated from the attitudes, values, perceptions, and feelings that both cause and result from it.

In fact, innovation appears to be a matter of values for many people. From an economic standpoint, innovation is typically considered to be good, if not ideal. In their best-seller *In Search of Excellence,* Thomas Peters and Robert Waterman define corporate excellence as "continuously innovative big companies."[23] From a societal standpoint, however, innovation may incur large costs, as opponents of nuclear energy and chemical pest control point out. Thus, although it is not socially acceptable to admit it in many quarters, some people view innovation negatively.[24]

The integrative approach to innovation taken in this book assumes that innovation is just one of many values that managers have, and that not all managers and companies value innovation equally highly. If it is valued highly by an organizations' top management, then it is likely to become a preferred means to some other ultimate end. If, on the other hand, it conflicts too sharply with values more highly prized by management (such as smooth quarterly earnings growth, cost reduction, or risk reduction), then innovation is not likely to be included among the organization's intermediate goals.

Most adults do not respond well to having someone else's values forced upon them. While debating values makes for interesting, emotional exchanges, it does not necessarily make for better decisions. Just as many behavioral science instructors explicitly refrain from imposing their values upon their students, while encouraging them to examine and clarify their own as value issues arise, so this book's intent is not to advocate that innovation is always good, and the larger and more radical the better. Rather, readers should decide for themselves whether innovation in general, its quantity, and its quality are good.

On the other hand, this approach to innovation presupposes that even more important than innovation itself is the ability to manage it, that is, to make good decisions about it so that (like fire, which can warm, but which can also burn) it can be kept constructive. The bias in this presentation, then, is that we need to make better decisions about innovation and that it is the quality of these decisions rather than innovation itself that is of paramount importance.

Critics of the prescriptions for improving innovation that call for earlier, more comprehensive, quantitative analysis (including sophisticated estimates of an innovation's risk) decry the rational approach as being too restrictive. That too much control stifles creativity has become the conventional wisdom. It should be noted that another assumption in the integrative approach is that pure rationality, if it could ever be achieved, does not necessarily produce the best decisions. Decisions that balance a variety of forces—such as intuition, values, and emotions, as well as reason—are believed to be "best" in this presentation.

Without quibbling about the actual nature of the decisions about innovation, however, it also should be noted that just as in counselling when the therapist's goal is to help clients to become aware of the causes and implications of particular behavior patterns and to become able to decide for themselves whether or not to engage in them, so the intent of this book is to help readers to clarify their own thinking about innovation, what it requires, and what it implies, so that they can make better decisions about it. Making better decisions about innovation should, in turn, lead to more effective performance in whatever way it is defined.

Conditions Fostering Innovation

In order for new things to be generated, adopted, or diffused, it is likely that a variety of conditions must be present. The following list is representative rather than exhaustive. Furthermore, there is no implication that all the conditions must be in place in order for innovation to occur. The following may be antecedents or maintainers of innovation, or both:

1. Perceived need for some better thing or for something that does not yet exist,[25]
2. Tolerance for uncertainty and ambiguity,[26]
3. Willingness to take risk,[27]
4. Belief in the value of new things in general,[28]
5. Belief in the ability to obtain valued benefits from the innovation,[29]
6. Participation in richly connected social networks,[30]
7. Willingness to experiment,[31] and
8. Willingness and ability to invest various kinds of resources in the new thing.[32]

These conditions are the attitudes and behaviors of individuals in larger contexts, such as groups, organizations, and societies. Like other attitudes and behaviors, these conditions exist along a continuum rather than as either/or occurrences. Thus, one may experience a greater or lesser *degree* of dissatisfaction, tolerance, or willingness.

To illustrate how the same condition can exist for different forms of innovation, the perceived dissatisfaction with something as it exists can be an antecedent to developing a new product or a new system. A designer who is dissatisfied with the efficiency of currently available wood-burning stoves may develop a new model with improved combustion capability or more aesthetic appearance. The management group of a company that suddenly finds itself with declining orders for its one product is likely to be willing to adopt a strategic planning system that it never had before in order to diversify. The group's dissatisfaction with its lack of planning as well as declining sales makes it more likely that it will take on a new administrative system.

The willingness to experiment is another case in point. It may be an important factor in determining whether or not a new thing, once conceived, is fully developed or completely adopted. This condition implies that it is acceptable to make mistakes if something can be learned from them. Experimentation is by nature a matter of trial and error. It can be as important to scientists bringing a new pharmaceutical to a level of sufficient safety and efficacy so that it can obtain U.S. Food and Drug Administration approval for introduction to the market, as it can be to information systems managers who are insuring that a new computer system actually does perform the functions that the company needs it to perform. If based on theories never before practiced, a new kind of educational organization probably will not survive if it is not willing to make adjustments in its curriculum or hiring practices as mistakes are made.

Universal Effects of Innovation

Just as some of the conditions conducive to innovation and the nature of innovation itself are similar for all of its forms, so, too, are some of its effects or outcomes. Whether the "something useful" resulting from the process of innovation is a product, service, set of procedures, or organizational form, it can have a variety of impacts on a variety of social systems.

For instance, developing a new product may change the way the firm's sales force presents its product line. Adopting a new operating procedure may require hiring more of a differently trained group of employees. Establishing a new form of health care provider, such as a health maintenance organization, may affect the employee benefits packages of a wide array of employers in a society. In each case, the innovation has implications not only for its original source, but also for its environment, in an ever-broadening series of repercussions.

All kinds of innovation, by definition, result in some kind of change, which can be described by an almost infinite number of dimensions. The change can also vary not only in its scope, but also in its degree. For instance, the development and adoption of the personal computer represents major differences in data processing for a broad spectrum of society, while the development and adoption of toothpaste with fluoride represents a relatively minor difference in dental hygiene. Of course, companies selling such toothpaste are unlikely to agree with this assessment.

Another common effect that all kinds of innovation have is that they elicit a range of attitudes from the people most involved in turning the new thing into something no longer new. If innovation leads to at least some degree of change, and if change causes at least some degree of disruption and modification of the existing order, then it should be expected that the people whose lives are disrupted are going to react in some way. Not all reactions and attitudes are negative despite the common assumption that people hate change and are basically conservative. Resistance to change is not automatic and universal. Indeed, it is ironic that innovation is commonly assumed to be a favorable occurrence and that change is commonly assumed to be a negative one. Yet, innovation implies change of some kind. Nonetheless, it is difficult to remain completely neutral toward new things, whatever they are.

Yet another outcome of innovation is that the new thing only remains new for a limited period of time. The newness is ever-diminishing as time progresses and as other new things emerge. Thus, the other effects, such as change in attitudes, may themselves change as the newness wears away from the fruits of the innovation process. A new procedure for serving customers becomes a comfortable routine after enough time and practice. A new kind of computer memory becomes old and obsolete as the most recent kind replaces it. This outcome of innovation, however, is most likely to occur if the innovation process achieves its purpose, which in itself can be considered an outcome.

The degree to which the results of the innovation process achieve their implicit or explicit objectives is an outcome common to all kinds of innovation. For instance, the return on investment (ROI) or share of the market (SOM) earned by a new product are certainly outcomes of innovation. The cost reduction, quality improvements, and productivity increases made possible by adopting CAD/CAM technology are also outcomes.

If any particular innovation process or specific useful new thing were to be evaluated, the above outcomes common to any kind of innovation would be potential criteria to use. Therefore, the degree to which the implications of the innovation were positive or negative for its source and its environment might be one way to assess an innovation's merit. The degree and scope of change engendered by the innovation, the attitudes of those people most affected by it, its duration as an innovation, and its ability to achieve its inherent purposes could all be applied to measure innovation in any form.

The ability to recognize these basic patterns, characteristic of all innovations' forms, should make it easier for top-level decision makers to know what kind of information they need in order to develop options and what kind of criteria they need to evaluate those options as they manage innovation. While actually making the choices is rarely easy, more generalist knowledge of the nature of innovation should give their decisions about it a better chance of benefitting their organizations as well as themselves.

Notes

1. National Science Foundation, *The Process of Technological Innovation: Reviewing the Literature* (Washington, D.C.: Government Printing Office, 1983).

2. Ibid.

3. C. Merle Crawford, *New Products Management* (Homewood, Ill.: Richard D. Irwin, 1983); and Edgar A. Pessemier, *Product Management: Strategy and Organization* (New York: John Wiley & Sons, 1982).

4. The terms *variation* and *reorientation* are used by Richard Normann, "Organizational Innovativeness: Product Variation and Reorientation," *Administrative Science Quarterly* (June 1971), pp. 203–15. The terms *evolution* and *revolution* are borrowed from executives at Polaroid Corporation and appear in Judith B. Kamm, *The Balance of Innovative Behavior and Control in New Product Development*, unpublished doctoral dissertation (Boston: Harvard University Graduate School of Business Administration, 1980).

5. John R. Kimberly, "Managerial Innovation," in P.C. Nystrom and W.H. Starbuck (eds.), *Handbook of Organizational Design* (London: Oxford University Press, 1981), pp. 84–104.

6. Michael E. Porter, "The Technological Dimension of Competitive Strategy," in Richard S. Rosenbloom (ed.), *Research on Technological Innovation, Management and Policy*, Vol. 1 (Greenwich, Conn: JAI Press, 1983), pp. 1–33.

7. Edgar A. Pessemier, *Product Management: Strategy and Organization* (New York: John Wiley & Sons, 1966).

8. Crawford, *New Products*.

9. H. Igor Ansoff and John M. Stewart, "Strategies for a Technology-Based Business," *Harvard Business Review*, 45 (November-December 1967), pp. 71–83; and Porter, "Technological Dimension."

10. Crawford, *New Products*.

11. Ibid.

12. Modesto A. Maidique and Peter Patch, "Corporate Strategy and Technological Policy," in Michael Tushman and William L. Moore (eds.), *Readings in the Management of Innovation* (Boston: Pitman, 1982), pp. 273–85.

13. Everett M. Rogers, *Diffusion of Innovations* (New York: Free Press, 1962).

14. Donald Schon, *Technology and Change* (New York: Delacorte, 1967).

15. William J. Abernathy and James M. Utterback, "Patterns of Industrial Innovation," *Technology Review*, 80 (1978), pp. 40–47.

16. Pessemier, *Product Management*, 1966, 1982; Porter, "Technological Dimension;" and Philip Marvin, *Product Planning Simplified* (New York: American Management Association, 1972).

17. Rogers, *Diffusion*.

18. Ibid.

19. Crawford, *New Products*.

20. Porter, "Technological Dimension."

21. Crawford, *New Products*.

22. National Science Foundation, *Process*, pp. 17, 22.

23. Thomas J. Peters and Robert H. Waterman, Jr., *In Search of Excellence* (New York: Harper & Row, 1982), p. 13.

24. Crawford, *New Products*, pp. 49–51; and Samuel C. Florman, *Blaming Technology: The Irrational Search for Scapegoats* (New York: St. Martin's, 1981).

25. A.K. Chakrabarti, "The Role of Champion in Product Innovation," *California Management Review*, Vol. 17, No. 2 (1974), pp. 58–62.

26. Jay W. Lorsch and John J. Morse, *Organizations and Their Members: A Contingency Approach* (New York: Harper & Row, 1974); and Paul R. Lawrence and Jay W. Lorsch, *Organization and Environment* (Homewood, Ill.: Richard D. Irwin, 1969).

27. Everett M. Rogers with Floyd F. Shoemaker, *Communication of Innovations: A Cross-Cultural Approach* (New York: Free Press, 1971); and National Science Foundation, *Process*, 1983.

28. T.S. Robertson, *Innovative Behavior and Communication* (New York: Holt, Rinehart and Winston, 1971).

29. Frederick E. Webster, Jr., *Industrial Marketing Strategy* (New York: John Wiley & Sons, 1979); and Pessemier, *Product Management*, 1982.

30. Michael L. Tushman, "Managing Communication Networks in R&D Laboratories," *Sloan Management Review*, Vol. 20 (Winter 1979), pp. 37–49; Robertson, *Innovative Behavior*; and Rogers and Shoemaker, *Communication of Innovations*.

31. Peters and Waterman, *In Search*; and Robertson, *Innovative Behavior*.

32. Webster, *Industrial Marketing Strategy*.

2
Innovation and Strategy

Organizational innovation is related to strategy in two important ways. On the one hand, innovation can be an essential objective or a means of achieving the long-term objectives that comprise the organization's mission. On the other hand, there can be goals for innovation itself and means for achieving these goals. That is, just as there is corporate or organizational strategy, so too can there be innovation strategy. Purists might prefer to call the latter "tactics," but whatever the term used, the basic idea is the same. This chapter explores both forms of the innovation–strategy relationship.

The Relationship between Innovation and Organizational Strategy

The commonality underlying most widely accepted definitions of organizational strategy is that of a consistent pattern of decisions about objectives and plans for achieving them. For example, decisions about what business the firm is in or is to be in[1] and about how to gain competitive advantage[2] are strategic. Adapting an organization to its environment is the main purpose or function of strategy.[3]

Innovation can be considered to be one type of long-range objective reflecting top management's or the dominant coalition's values and aspirations.[4] This objective may then appear in more concrete, short-run terms at lower organizational levels, such as divisions and strategic business units. Whereas corporate strategy defines the boundaries of which business the organization is to be in, divisional or business-level strategy defines the way in which it will compete within a given business.[5] Examples of business-level goals are the development of particular products or services, the opening of specific new markets, and the establishment of major R&D projects.[6]

Indeed, assuming that organizational goals form a means–ends hierarchy,[7] with corporate- or organizational-level objectives at the top, the link between strategy and innovation is clear. Generating and/or adopting useful new things—innovation—is one of many possible means for achieving such ends as growth in sales, maintenance of market share, technological leadership, and long-term profitability, even survival.[8] Conversely, the nature of these more ultimate ends has been assumed here to act as a set of boundaries or constraints upon innovation,[9] that is, the context for it.

In studying or making decisions about a particular new thing, for a variety of reasons it is important to take into account the innovating unit's strategic context. Just to understand what happens as a new idea develops requires knowledge about what else is occurring—or is supposed to occur—in the organizational unit.[10] Its strategy can be not only a significant determinant of its personnel's ability, but also of its management's willingness to innovate.

A unit's ability to innovate involves the expertise of its people about the kind of innovation it is plus the existence of the required physical materials, equipment, and space. The willingness of a unit's management to innovate is based on its attitudes and perceptions of the importance of the need to do so relative to other needs, such as expanding facilities, cost cutting, or increasing advertising or distribution support for existing products or services. Overall strategy, then, often determines how much of the unit's resources are made available for the innovation. Resource allocation can play an important role in when, how rapidly, and/or how extensively something new develops or is adopted.[11]

Using the Classification Scheme

The following analysis of organizational strategy is intended to deepen understanding of the concept itself and its essential link to innovation. Table 2–1 presents the important dimensions of strategy in a classification scheme similar to the one used for innovation in table 1–1. Ultimately, both of these schemes will be juxtaposed in order to provide an integrative framework for either identifying existing innovation strategies or consciously selecting one to use.

The framework in table 2–1 integrates a number of other, more limited typologies.[12] It attempts to capture the complexity of strategy as well as to permit managers to more easily plan and researchers to more precisely describe it. Because there is no assumption that strategy is always predetermined, however, this framework can be used to identify a particular strategy after the fact.

Strategy can be viewed as having four dimensions: organizational level, nature of product(s) or services(s), the market(s) environment, and goal orientation. Resource allocation has not been included as a dimension of strategy itself, although it is commonly conceptualized as such.[13] In this presentation, however, resource allocation is considered to be a way of putting strategy into effect, a result rather than a dimension of strategy itself.

Table 2–1
Types of Strategy: A Classification Scheme

Organizational level:
  Corporate
  Group (divisions and/or geographic territories)
  Divisional (businesses and/or territories)
  Business (industry, market, market segment)
  Functional (R&D, marketing, production/operations, personnel, finance)

Nature of products or services:
  Relationship among them
    Integration (forward or backward)
    Diversification
  Nature of competitive advantage (cost, quality, availability, and so forth)
  Performance (volume, margin, market share, strength of unit, cost, and so forth)

Market environment:
  Dynamism
    Stability (static/changing)
    Rate of growth
  Scope of relative to organization (narrow/broad)
  Attractiveness to organization
    Competitive structure
    Rate of technological advance
    Regulation

Goal orientation:
  Intended/unintended
  Realized/unrealized

Organizational Level

If strategy is a pattern of decisions about organizational objectives and plans for achieving them, then the first identifying feature of any strategy must be the location of the decision makers within the organization. What level of the hierarchy has ultimate responsibility for approving or making decisions and for insuring that they are carried out? Early work on the concept of strategy focussed on the most general, top-level corporate managers' decision making.[14] Toward the end of the 1970s, however, more attention began to be paid to what the divisions or business units of diversified firms were doing and how that related to the strategy at corporate headquarters.[15]

The definition of strategy as a pattern of decisions about organizational objectives and plans for achieving them is general enough, however, to be interpreted as unit or departmental objectives and plans rather than being restricted to divisional and corporate levels. At the more specialized levels of the marketing and R&D functions, for example, the market or environment surrounding the unit may be thought of as consisting of the other units of the organization. Just as the organization as a whole relates to its entire market or domain, so each of its units, however defined, relates to the entire organization. In the absence of a clearly formed top-level strategy for the whole organization, in fact, the strategy of each of its main functions may be the only clue to what the entire entity may or may not do. In other words, the assumption that each unit is completely constrained by the goals and plans of the next larger unit encompassing it may not be valid and is not made here.

It may not always be clear who has the authority to make strategic decisions. If it is not clear, the next step is to examine the content of the decisions themselves. In other words, what kinds of decisions are being designed or explained? If they have anything to do with either product/service or market issues, then the degree to which the organization is diversified can be an important indicator of the organizational level at which the strategy applies.

That is, if the organization only operates in one industry and the decisions are about what industry or country to enter, remain in, or leave, it is usually corporate- or top-level strategy. If the decisions are about what position to take within an industry, or what specific part of an industry to operate in, it also may be a top-level decision. If, however, the organization is diversified into more than one industry, then these decisions may be at the group or divisional level. If a diversified, divisionalized organization does business in more than one part of an industry and, thus, has several product lines within it, most decisions about any one product line would be made by either divisional or business unit management, if a division is large enough to have more than one business unit.

Finally, at the functional level of either a diversified or undiversified organization, departmental management usually makes decisions about how a particular product or service is to be made, provided, or sold. Thus, the marketing vice president may ultimately decide how a product is advertised or priced. The R&D vice president may ultimately decide which new-product projects will be funded for further development in any given period.

Once it has been determined what the decisions comprising the strategy are about and who is making them, it is necessary to fill in the content details of the goals and plans. The product/service nature and market environment dimensions are the vehicle for describing the substance of the strategy itself. Thus, information about each of the three features of the nature dimension and each of the three features of the market dimension should be obtained.

The Nature of Product(s) or Service(s)

In order to adequately describe and explain the nature of an organization's product or service (in other words, what it does), three important features of it must be considered: how it relates to what else the organization produces or provides; how it is better than or different from comparable things done by the organization's competitors; and how well it achieves the organization's overall objectives. Each of these aspects will be discussed in the following sections.

Relationship among Products or Services. A number of experts have identified and categorized the ways in which business organizations typically branch out from the one product that they originally made and sold.[16] The branching has taken two predominant forms: vertical integration or diversification. Vertical integration either can be backward into the production of materials or equipment supplying the original product, or it can be forward into the production of the output or end product requiring the original product as a component. Diversification can be into either a product with a similar technology and market or else one with a completely different technology and market.

Nature of Products' or Services' Competitive Advantage. Whatever makes a product or service discernably better or different from others like it gives it its advantage over them with buyers or users, thus enabling it to compete effectively. Cost, quality, availability, ease of use, durability, styling, and versatility of the product or service itself are among the features that are valued more or less by various parts of the market. Competitive advantage, however, is a very broad term. It encompasses all of the ways that an organization uses its products to perform as well as, if not to dominate, the other organizations in its industry. Hence, this feature of a product or service directs one's attention to the industry, not from the point of view of the buyers, but rather from that of the sellers.[17]

Products' or Services' Performance. Much of the empirical research[18] and prescriptive work[19] on business strategy has used performance data such as volume, market share, profitability, and growth to describe and measure strategy. Because these are measures of the results of a particular strategy, this approach to identifying and categorizing strategy as a phenomenon does not concern itself with how and why strategy is formed, but rather only with the degree of effectiveness with which organizational goals are being achieved.

Market(s) Environment

As previously mentioned, strategy is the way in which an organization relates to its environment. Indeed, most of the major typologies of strategy include some feature of the market environment as a key dimension. The dynamism, attractiveness, and scope of the market relative to the organization are three of the most important aspects of the market environment discussed in the following sections.

Dynamism. This term refers to the amount of change, including the rate of growth, in an organization's domain. Raymond Miles and Charles Snow view this variable as the leading one in their typology of ways in which to move through the "adaptive cycle."[20] This cycle consists of finding solutions to three different kinds of problems: the "entrepreneurial problem" of defining concretely the product-market domain, the "engineering problem" of selecting appropriate systems and technology for producing and distributing the product that solve the entrepreneurial problem, and the "administrative problem" of routinizing the successful solutions to the problems encountered during the two earlier phases.

Firms' strategies (ways of solving these problems) can be categorized into four types. Defenders are firms using the strategy of remaining in relatively stable domains experiencing little technological or competitive change. Analyzers are firms whose strategy is to be in both stable and changing markets, while prospectors only position themselves in changing markets. They initiate change, forcing their competitors to respond. Reactors are firms that do just as their name suggests. Their strategy is not clearly discernable, and they are slow to respond to changes in their domain, unlike defenders.[21]

The growth rate of a market that an organization relates to is another form of dynamism that has been used to characterize strategy. Definitions and measures of growth in markets vary, and a detailed presentation is beyond the scope of this book. However, 10 percent or greater growth per year is generally considered a high rate.[22]

Scope. The scope of an organization's particular market environment is the comprehensiveness of the way in which it defines its domain. How narrowly or how broadly is it conceptualized? "Defenders"[23] or dominant-business firms[24] have a narrow market definition enabling them to remain within their proven managerial and technical expertise. "Prospectors," on the other hand, very broadly define their domain, permitting them to range about, seeking new opportunities for rapid growth. They are, by definition, diversified.[25]

Attractiveness of the Market to the Organization. Yet another feature of organizations' market environments is their desirability, which includes such characteristics as size, pricing, diversity, competitive structure, and profitability, as well as technological, social, and legal factors.[26] Industry attractiveness, of course, is perceptual in that it depends on the nature of the organization assessing it.

Goal Orientation

The final dimension of strategy is more of a process than a content dimension because it captures the way in which a strategy was or is being formed, and the degree to which it is being or has been brought to fruition. Mintzberg's typology, incorporated in table 2–1, consists of two dimensions: (1) the degree to which goals and plans have been consciously decided upon or intended by an organization's management and (2) the degree to which these goals and plans have been implemented or realized as a consistent pattern in a stream of decisions.[27] The four strategies resulting from the juxtaposition of these dimensions are: failed or "intended unrealized"; "deliberate" or intended realized; "emergent" or unintended realized; and "unintended unrealized", which is no discernable pattern of decisions at all or a lack of strategy.

An intended strategy is the conscious establishment of basic long-term objectives. It is made in advance of the specific decision to which it applies; thus, it forms a set of a priori guidelines. An unintended strategy, on the other hand, is implicit. It evolves, consisting of a posteriori decisions made one by one. Realized strategy is a consistent sequence in a stream of decisions representing commitment, usually of resources, to action. Unrealized strategy presents no discernable pattern. An organization's behavior appears to have no goals and, thus, to be random.

Knowledge about any of these four dimensions should help to explain the others as well as to act as guidelines for the shape that a strategy in the making should take. As mentioned above, the extent to which an organization diversifies its products or services can be an important starting place for identifying and describing its strategy. Not only can it provide an indication of what level of management is or should be making the decisions comprising the strategy, but it can also provide an indicator of how difficult it is to use simple, summary terms to capture the essence of an organization's strategy.

The more diversified an organization is, the more difficult it is to go beyond this one descriptor. Indeed, to do so, it becomes necessary to name each of the businesses in which it is engaged and to use the three nature features and the three market environment features to describe each business.

If diversification is an "emergent strategy," there may be little connection among the businesses, making it difficult to make sense of what, if anything, all the data mean. Thus, there may appear to be no organizing principles to aid in description and classification. The further up the organization one moves away from the details of the disparate businesses and toward the overall strategy of diversification, the more blurred and indistinguishable labels become.

Portfolio or Focussed Strategy?

One approach to organizing diversification that has been widely recommended by theoreticians and used by managers during the past decade is the portfolio approach. Taken from financial investment theory, in which the objective is to maximize return while minimizing risk of investments, the portfolio approach to managing diversification is best represented by the Boston Consulting Group market share/market growth matrix. Businesses can be categorized as cows, dogs, problem children, or stars, enabling management to keep track not so much of its risk (although risk is related to cash availability), but rather of its cash—which businesses it comes from and which businesses are consuming it.[28]

In general, adopting a portfolio strategy may mean that management is aware of its strengths and weaknesses, and that it is using its strengths to counterbalance its short-term weaknesses in order to at least attempt to strengthen or compensate for them over the long term as well. The portfolio concept has also found a wide variety of applications in contexts characterized by conflicting needs or values. Its basic function is to permit a balancing of these contrarieties, whatever they are, including short term versus long term, risk versus return, and efficiency versus innovation.

A portfolio strategy, then, is one in which there is a consistent pattern of decisions about apparently contradictory objectives and plans for achieving them. If the organization's management, at whatever level it is making decisions, looks as if it wants to have its cake and to eat it, too, then it probably is adopting a portfolio strategy. The opposite kind of strategy is one in which objectives are complementary rather than contradictory. If the organization's management looks as if it is putting all of its cake in one basket, then a focussed strategy is probably in effect.

Innovation Strategy

Many companies have had an innovation strategy to a certain extent for years without either making it explicit or formal, or labelling it in any particular way.[29] It has usually been outsiders, either researchers or industry analysts, who have noticed patterns in companies' innovation. Yet, these patterns have only been described in the most general terms, such as calling firms "habitually first to the market."[30]

Innovation strategy is the pattern of decisions about the types of new things generated or adopted. This definition is general enough to encompass both major forms of innovation: generation and adoption. It also includes not only deliberate decisions made before innovation actually occurs, but also unplanned decisions made after it occurs. Defining innovation strategy at this level of abstraction also permits an individual or group in any functional specialty (such as R&D, marketing, or management information systems) or at any hierarchical level of the organization to use it. Such generality is necessary because decisions about innovation are made at different levels and by a variety of functional specialties in different organizations.

The pattern of decisions comprising innovation strategy takes the form of a set of goals and plans for innovation. As in organizational strategy, this pattern is held together by an underlying logic of means and ends. For example, a firm's top management may have the following reasons for innovating: it can only maintain market share in its industry by doing so; it can only maintain profitability by keeping market share; and, furthermore, it takes pride in its past innovativeness and does not want to damage its image.

These reasons for innovating in turn contribute to the goals that any new idea must promise to achieve in order to be further developed for introduction to the market or adoption by the organization. Therefore, the goal of x degrees of acceptance by the current market becomes important. In order to gain this degree of market acceptance, certain limitations may come into play that themselves become goals. For example, if past experience in this market indicates that it rejects anything beyond price y, then cost levels become goals for new ideas to achieve.

At the same time, the innovation must promise enough of an advantage over what is currently available in the market to at least prevent loss of market share and ideally to gain it. Providing a significant advantage over what exists also achieves the goal of keeping an organizational image of innovativeness. Given the company's cost and profit structure and the nature of the innovation, the acceptable ways of developing the new thing to meet the above goals may themselves be limited. In other words, the plans for innovation may follow closely from the goals.

The plans for this innovation must balance the need for a significant advantage with the need for minimal cost. One way of reducing development costs is to reduce the amount of new-idea testing that is done. If the new idea is similar enough to something extremely new that has already been introduced or adopted, benefits can be gained from learning about other organizations' experience. At the same time, the new idea can be made sufficiently different from what already exists by being tailored specifically to the unique needs of a segment of the market or to the needs of the adopting firm.

This example is greatly simplified in its assumption of a rational chain of cause and effect, one new idea, one market, and one industry. Nonetheless, it does uncover the outline of what an innovation strategy is. The basic elements of this framework will be used further on in the chapter to explain a more complicated portfolio strategy for innovation.

It should be noted that if, when, and how a firm innovates is not always planned. Thus, the chain of events comprising its strategy may come from such things as managers' responses to serendipitous discoveries and environmental "accidents" and threats. In such cases, the pattern of decisions only becomes apparent after the decisions are made and compared to other managerial decisions about innovation.

Identifying Types of Innovation Strategy

Juxtaposing the schemes for classifying innovation and classifying strategy is one method for identifying a particular kind of innovation strategy. Table 2–2 vis-

Table 2–2
Types of Innovation Strategy: A Classification Scheme

Organizational level:
    Corporate or top

    Group

    Divisional

    Business unit

    Functional

Nature of organizational level's products or services:
    Relationship among them (diversified or integrated)

    Competitive advantage (cost, quality, availability, and so forth)

    Performance (volume, market share, margin, cost, and so forth)

Market environment:
    Dynamism (stability or growth)

    Scope (narrow or broad)

    Attractiveness to organization (competitive structure, technological advance, regulation, and so forth)

Form of innovation:
    Generation or adoption of technological product, process, or service

    Generation or adoption of market for product or service

    Generation or adoption of organizational structure or procedure

Function of innovation:
    Improves quality

    Reduces cost

    Performs functions not previously performed

    Enhances attractiveness for current market

    Increases offerings to current market

    Enters market not currently served

    Improves learning curve

    Enhances economies of scale

    Permits production of better-quality offering

    Enhances human growth and development

Extent of innovation ($0°-180°$)

Timing of innovation:
    First-to-market (or first-to-adopt)

    Quick second

    Quick third

    Late follower

Goal orientation:
    Intended/unintended

    Realized/unrealized

ually represents this synthesis. Moving from top to bottom, the first three dimensions (the organizational level of decision making, the nature of that level's product or service, and its market environment) provide a description of the existing strategic context within which decisions about innovation are made.

The next four dimensions (the nature, function, extent, and timing of the innovation) provide a description of the decisions made about it. Finally, the goal-orientation dimension permits an assessment of the decision-making process.

In using the scheme, it does not really matter where classification begins, although two likely choices are the organizational level and the nature of the innovation. In order to fully describe any given pattern of decisions about innovation, however, data along every dimension should be obtained. In order to demonstrate how this typology works, examples of the two most general innovation strategies, focussed and portfolio, will be presented next.

Focussed Innovation Strategy

A focussed innovation strategy is one in which the decisions are about one predominant kind of innovation, as determined by its nature, function, extent, or timing or by all four of these dimensions. For example, one silverware company's only form of innovation was to make lower-priced copies of competitors' new products. Pricing was always its chief competitive weapon. Only the less-expensive materials, lower-cost manufacturing process, and correspondingly lower price were new. Management's definition of innovation was those items that had never been made by the company before.

Applying the dimensions of the innovation strategy classification scheme in table 2–2 to this case produces the following summary. Corporate-level decisions about innovation in this dominant-business (undiversified) firm were made well within its overall strategy of being a price-leader among its competitors. This approach enabled it to gain a significant share of its expanding market, which was narrowly defined as price-conscious consumers of flatware and giftware. This market was attractive because few firms competed in it, and there was little technological advancement. Innovation consisted of generating close imitations of other firms' new products that served the function for the company of increasing offerings to its current market and of enhancing the products' price attractiveness for its current market. Thus, it was a high-volume manufacturer of products new only to the company and to the lower-price–range market segment. This was its intended, realized innovation strategy.

Portfolio Innovation Strategy

Clearly, it is easier to identify a consistent pattern of decisions when they are about one type of innovation than it is to make sense of decisions about many kinds of innovation. The portfolio strategy for innovation was discovered when, in selecting a sample of high technology divisions in which to study new-product development, an unsuccessful attempt was made to identify and categorize them according to the extent of their innovation (revolutionary or evolutionary).

The research attempted to compare the ways in which the two types of divisions managed their scientists or engineers who actually developed new products. The expectation was that divisions with a strategy of generating radically new products would manage their researchers differently from those divisions with a strategy of generating not-so-new products. When the investigation started, however, innovation strategy per se was not a recognized construct. Therefore, no earlier attempts to describe it systematically had been made. No comprehensive typologies of innovation, strategy, or innovation strategy such as appear in tables 1–1, 2–1, and 2–2 yet existed. In fact, measuring and classifying divisional strategies continues to be problematic.[31]

Nevertheless, based primarily upon their corporate R&D-to-sales ratios, seven divisions that agreed to participate in the study were selected. Semiconductor company A was expected to have a revolutionary new-product strategy, while evolutionary strategies were expected in semiconductor companies B and C. In 1977, their ratios were 8.2, 5.9, and 3.7, respectively. Pharmaceuticals companies D, E, and F had high R&D expenditure-to-sales ratios of 8.2, 9.0, and 7.9, respectively. Company G's ratio was 3.3. Therefore, it was anticipated that companies D, E, and F would have revolutionary strategies and that company G would have an evolutionary strategy.

Table 2–3 contains the interview questions asked of division general managers or their counterparts. The items are grouped into four general descriptors of innovation strategy: (1) general management's definition of innovation, (2) management's objectives for innovation, (3) resources supporting innovation, and (4) the division's actual innovation, including its innovative stance in its industry. It was anticipated that management's "intended strategy," as reflected in the first three items in table 2–3, might diverge from its "realized strategy," as reflected in the last seven items.[32]

Strategies change over time and some divisions were expected to be in a transition phase. Thus, a division with an intended revolutionary innovation strategy and a realized evolutionary strategy would not have been a surprise. In fact, the method of personally interviewing managers, using a broad range of measures, was originally intended to capture just such a phenomenon.

The following features were originally believed to indicate a revolutionary innovation strategy:

1. Innovation defined as a significant advance in the state of the art,

2. Innovation sought for its own sake or to insure leadership in industry, not for high percentage of future sales growth,

3. Few specific commercial constraints such as return on investment or pay-back hurdles,

4. Relatively high percentage of staff working primarily on basic research or developing radically new products,

5. Moderate to high percentage of past year's sales derived from products introduced in past five years,

6. Moderate number of new products introduced in past five years, and

7. Division usually being first to the market with new products.

The assumptions underlying these measures of revolutionary innovation are that such innovation by nature cannot be relied upon to generate sales and profits at any predictable level within any predictable time period, that radical innovation occurs infrequently, and that radical innovation requires significant amounts of monetary and human resources.

If a division scored low on these features, it was judged to have an evolutionary strategy. Self-typing, competitors' assessments, and investigator inferences were used to determine whether divisional strategies were revolutionary, evolutionary, or "mixed" according to these measures.[33]

A comparison of the data in table 2–3 against the above descriptors indicates that not only did no company have either an intended or realized revolutionary strategy, but that only company A had a purely evolutionary intended strategy. In all other companies, both intended and realized strategies combined features of both revolutionary and evolutionary innovation.

Company A's realized strategy appears to have more traits of radical innovation than would be expected from its management's definition of and goals for innovation. The same may be said for companies B and G. At the time of the study, companies A, B, and F were improving recent breakthroughs. Company B was also preparing to introduce another breakthrough in another product line. Company G was more than two years from introducing a breakthrough cardiovascular drug, hence its high resource allocation figures. Thus, the measures of intended and realized strategies may be discrepant because of the time lag between them.

In addition to these discrepancies, there appears to be a mixture of types of innovation indicated within these companies' intended strategies as well as within their realized strategies. That few divisions' managers intended to have either a purely revolutionary or evolutionary strategy is evidenced by their definitions of innovation. With the exception of those in companies A and D, they included both revolutionary and evolutionary terms.

Furthermore, even if, as in company D, innovation is conceptualized in revolutionary terms, new products must nonetheless promise to meet quantitative standards of sales and market share before they are developed enough to

Table 2–3
Innovation Strategy in Seven High Technology Divisions

Descriptors	Semiconductor Companies				Ethical Pharmaceutical Companies		
	Company A	Company B	Company C	Company D	Company E	Company F	Company G
I. Intended strategy							
A. General management's definition of innovation	e (improving existing products and using existing concepts to perform new functions; second sourcing)	m (developing new proprietary items creating new market or requiring new production facility; improving existing products, often defined by special users)	m (developing products able to perform new electronic function or manufacturing smaller, improved versions of current products)	r (developing products that are very new and never before seen or characterized chemically)	m (developing radically new chemical entities never before on market, products of any advantage to user, or products that reduce risk or insure compliance with FDA; using old products for new ailments)	m (developing products that are rare among the rare or else new to the company but already in the market)	m (developing truly unique drug entities or improved products)
B. Innovation objectives							
1. Percentage of future growth in sales expected from new products?	e (100%)	e (80%)	r (30%)	NA	e (85%)	r (50%)	NA
2. Preestablished ROI, SOM, payback, or other hurdles new products must meet?	e (average of $1 million annual sales for 3 years)	r (use existing manufacturing technology and engineering resources; product inexpensive to make)	e (high sales; stepingstone to other new products; figure of merit = estimated revenue ÷ costs)	e ($80–150 million annual sales and SOM)	e (positive ROI averaging 25% over life cycle; $100 million annual sales)	e (return on marketing investment; sufficient gross margin; cost of chemicals and production)	e (production cost of necessary dosage for efficacy; profitability; SOM; first-year sales; cost of goods sold; capital expenses; ROI)
II. Realized strategy							
A. Resources supporting innovation							

1. Percentage of division's annual sales revenue spent on product development?	r (8–9%)	r (10%)	e (5–10%)	r (8–9%)	r (10%)	e (7–8%)	r (13%)
2. Percentage of division's R&D staff work spent solely on radically new products?	NA	r (34%)	NA	e (20%)	e (20–25%)	NA	r (40%)
B. Division's actual innovation							
1. Percentage of last year's sales and earnings from products introduced within past five years?	r (60–70%)	r (100%)	r (100%)	NA	e (40% sales/25% earnings)	r (60%)	e (20–25%)
2. Number of products introduced in past five years?	r (150–200)	e (300–400)	r (50)	r (5)	e (15)	r (3)	e (12)
3. Percentage of products that were radically new?	NA	e (.13%)	NA	NA	r (33%)	r (60%)	e (15%)
4. Percentage of radically new products that failed?	NA	e (.02%)	NA	NA	e (30%)	r (0)	e (20%)
5. Which company is usually first to the market with new products?	m ("This is too broad an industry to have one answer.")	e (Intel is first. Company B and Texas Instruments are usually second.")	m ("It depends on which segment.")	r (Company D)	m ("There is no typical company. Companies specialize and there are oligopolies in these categories.")	m ("Company F is a specialty house. We use the Boston Consulting Group idea and it frustrates researchers.")	NA

Notes: r = revolutionary innovation strategy; e = evolutionary innovation strategy; m = mixed strategy; NA = not available.

be submitted to the Food and Drug Administration, the final step before market introduction. In fact, only companies B and F had the kind of general constraints that can sometimes paradoxically stimulate breakthroughs by setting parameters within which new-product ideas must be generated and problems solved.

It should be noted that despite their relatively general constraints, however, companies B and F did not define innovation solely in revolutionary terms. There appears to be a balancing of what extent of innovation management wants and the degree of risk it is willing to take to get it. Balancing is also apparent in most companies' realized strategies as indicated by their responses to the question about their innovative stance in their industries.

The managers in companies A, C, E, and F believed that in order to determine whether a company has a first-to-market strategy or not, it is necessary to specify narrowly a product line or market segment. Because all divisions studied made several product lines for a variety of market segments, even if they were first to the market with some parts of their business, they were not and did not intend to be first with the rest of it. Therefore, managers of all companies except B and D were reluctant to generalize about their strategies to the extent assumed possible in existing typologies of innovation.

Formulating Portfolio Strategies of Innovation

A mixture of types of innovation, as measured by its extent or degree of newness, was apparent in all seven companies studied. Therefore, an either/or approach to innovation appears to be too crude to accurately portray the reality of firms' divisional strategies. At this level, strategies tend to fall somewhere in between and are multidimensional in nature.

It is likely that the companies studied did not try to be and were not first to the market in all their product lines or market segments because of the inherent uncertainty of doing so. Three types of uncertainty have been identified. Technical uncertainty is the lack of information about how well the innovation will meet a variety of criteria without significantly increasing costs. Market uncertainty is lack of data about the likelihood that other firms will either introduce the new thing first or quickly copy it, stealing market share before market dominance can be attained by the leader. Business uncertainty is lack of knowledge about general economic trends. Because technical and market uncertainty can never be eliminated entirely, most firms have strong reasons for minimizing the extent of their innovation unless they are large and can afford to cushion such uncertainty with investment in safer innovation projects.[34]

All of the divisions studied support this conclusion. Clear examples of the portfolio approach to balancing the risks of innovation appeared in company F (whose management explicitly referred to the Boston Consulting Group's model) and in company D, whose laboratory president also explicitly described its innovation strategy as consisting of both revolutionary and evolutionary projects.

In addition to having a portfolio of radically new and not-so-new products simultaneously under development, divisions may also balance degrees of innovation sequentially over time. Divisions whose products, such as pharmaceuticals, have long life cycles, may shift most of their resources to a breakthrough when it comes and then concentrate upon improving it or finding new uses for it until the next revolution occurs.

The portfolio strategy of innovation, then, should be useful for divisionalized organizations having diversified products or services across industries, or undiversified companies or divisions having a variety of product lines within a broadly defined industry such as integrated circuit semiconductors.

The purpose of a portfolio is to minimize risk while maximizing return by spreading risk out across a variety of investments. Therefore, the portfolio concept may be extended to the adoption of innovation as well. Using very new technologies, techniques, or markets in some businesses or product lines may be balanced off with retaining familiar technologies, techniques, or markets in others.[35]

The portfolio concept in product planning in general is not new. It has been recommended by marketing theorists for managing existing, rather than new, product lines. Three steps have been suggested for creating any kind of portfolio. First, determine unit objectives and the trade-offs between them, such as risk versus return or market share versus cost reduction. Next, evaluate each item (product, process, or service) in terms of the degree to which it meets the portfolio objectives. Finally, balance the portfolio. That is, some items may need to be reduced or increased; more resources may be allocated to some items and fewer to others. Actually taking these steps, however, may be more difficult than anticipated.[36]

Another approach to formulating a portfolio of innovations is the development of "product innovation charters" or PICs for each very specific product line, such as toys for pets as distinguished from flea powder. These charters represent each new product's strategy. They are comprised of three major elements: (1) strategic arena, including product type, end-user application, customer group, and technology, (2) goals of the new-product activity, including growth, market status, and special purposes, and (3) the program to achieve the goals, including the organizational location of the innovative element, the degree of innovativeness used, timing of market entry, and such special dimensions as regulatory avoidance, product quality level, and patentability.[37,38]

The Importance of Innovation Strategy

No matter what kind of innovation strategy is used, there are several reasons why it is worth formulating. It increases managers' awareness of what they want to accomplish, what their options are for what they can do, and what their units' strengths and weaknesses are. Formulating strategy forces managers to pay attention to their competitors and regulators as well as to other salient features of their companies' environments. With this heightened awareness and increased information, managers can make better decisions, not only in advance planning, but also as the need for innovation decisions arises. Decisions based upon better information and more careful consideration of alternatives and consequences increase managers' degree of control over the kind of activity, in this case innovation, for which the strategy is formulated.

Better decisions about specific innovations of any kind, including new organizational structures and systems, can minimize expensive failures and losses that waste resources, thereby making them available for more promising ideas. Fewer failures avoid souring organizational members' attitudes toward taking the kinds of personal risks necessary to maintain the flow of new ideas. Of course, because uncertainty is inherent to innovation, it is unrealistic to think that better decision making can entirely prevent mistakes and failures. It can, however, direct and protect the innovation process so that it can flourish when top management wants it to do so.

Finally, it is important to formulate innovation strategy so that those who come up with and develop new ideas know why new ideas are needed. A sense of purpose makes it easier to evaluate innovations during their unfolding and on this basis to allocate sufficient resources to them. Strategy can reduce some of the organizational uncertainty faced by innovators, thereby freeing them to focus more of their energies on their new ideas. Innovation strategy provides a framework of managerial control within which innovators are free to explore and experiment.

Notes

1. Kenneth Andrews, *The Concept of Corporate Strategy* (Homewood, Ill.: Dow Jones-Irwin, 1971).

2. George S. Day, "A Strategic Perspective on Product Planning," *Journal of Contemporary Business* (Spring 1975), pp. 1–34.

3. Raymond E. Miles and Charles E. Snow, *Organizational Strategy, Structure, and Process* (New York: McGraw-Hill, 1978); and Henry Mintzberg, "Patterns in Strategy Formation," *Management Science*, Vol. 24, No. 9 (May 1978).

4. Yoram J. Wind, *Product Policy: Concepts, Methods, and Strategy* (Reading, Mass.: Addison-Wesley, 1982).

5. Dan E. Schendel and Charles W. Hofer, *Strategic Management: A New View of Business Policy and Planning* (Boston: Little, Brown, 1979).

6. Kalman J. Cohen and Richard M. Cyert, "Strategy Formulation, Implementation, and Monitoring," *Journal of Business*, 46 (July 1973), pp. 349–67.

7. Herbert A. Simon, *Administrative Behavior: A Study of Decision-Making in Administrative Organizations*, 3rd. ed. (New York: Free Press, 1976); George Steiner, *Top Management Planning* (New York: Macmillan, 1969); and Wind, *Product Policy*.

8. Peter F. Drucker, *The Practice of Management* (New York: Harper & Row, 1954); Frank Hull and Jerald Hage, "Innovative Payoff from R&D," paper presented at the Academy of Management Annual Meeting, New York, 1982; and Robert R. Rothberg (ed.), *Corporate Strategy and Product Innovation*, 2nd ed. (New York: Free Press, 1981).

9. Johannes M. Pennings and Paul S. Goodman, "Toward a Workable Framework," in Paul S. Goodman and Johannes M. Pennings and Associates, *New Perspectives on Organizational Effectiveness* (San Francisco: Jossey-Bass, 1977); and Schendel and Hofer, *Strategic Management*.

10. Richard S. Rosenbloom, "Technological Innovation in Firms and Industries: An Assessment of the State of the Art," Working Paper No. 74–8 (Boston: Harvard University Graduate School of Business Administration, April 1974).

11. Everett M. Rogers with Floyd F. Shoemaker, *Communication of Innovations: A Cross-Cultural Approach* (New York: Free Press, 1971).

12. Bruce D. Henderson, *Henderson on Corporate Strategy* (New York: Mentor, 1979); Miles and Snow, *Organizational Strategy*; Michael E. Porter, *Competitive Strategy: Techniques for Analyzing Industries and Competitors* (New York: Free Press, 1980); and Richard Rumelt, *Strategy, Structure, and Economic Performance* (Boston: Division of Research, Harvard University Graduate School of Business Administration, 1974).

13. Henderson, *Corporate Strategy*; and Porter, *Competitive Strategy*.

14. Andrews, *Concept*; Alfred D. Chandler, *Strategy and Structure* (Cambridge, Mass.: MIT Press, 1962); Henderson, *Corporate Strategy*; and Rumelt, *Strategy*.

15. Cohen and Cyert, "Strategy Formulation"; Donald C. Hambrick, Ian C. MacMillan, and D.L. Day, "Strategic Attributes and Performance in the BCG Matrix—A PIMS Based Analysis of Industrial-Product Businesses," *Academy of Management Review*, Vol. 5., No. 4 (1980), pp. 567–75; Schendel and Hofer, *Strategic Management*; and Richard Vancil, *Decentralization: Managerial Ambiguity by Design* (New York: Financial Executives Research Foundation, 1980).

16. Chandler, *Strategy and Structure*; Rumelt, *Strategy*; and Leonard Wrigley, "Divisional Autonomy and Diversification," unpublished doctoral dissertation (Boston: Harvard University Graduate School of Business Administration, 1970).

17. Porter, *Competitive Strategy*.

18. Vasudevan Ramanujam and N. Venkatraman, "An Inventory and Critique of Strategy Research Using the PIMS Database," *Academy of Management Review*, Vol. 9, No. 1 (1984), pp. 138–51.

19. Henderson, *Corporate Strategy*; and Porter, *Competitive Strategy*.

20. Miles and Snow, *Organizational Strategy*.

21. Ibid.

22. Henderson, *Corporate Strategy*.

23. Miles and Snow, *Organizational Strategy*.

24. Rumelt, *Strategy*.

25. Miles and Snow, *Organizational Strategy*.

26. Porter, *Competitive Strategy*.

27. Mintzberg, "Patterns."

28. Henderson, *Corporate Strategy*.

29. Merle C. Crawford, *New Products Management* (Homewood, Ill.: Richard D. Irwin, 1983).

30. H. Igor Ansoff and John M. Stewart, "Strategies for a Technology-Based Busi-

ness," *Harvard Business Review,* Vol. 45 (November-December 1967), pp. 71–83; and Modesto A. Maidique and Peter Patch, "Corporate Strategy and Technological Policy," in Michael Tushman and William L. Moore (eds.), *Readings in the Management of Innovation* (Boston: Pitman, 1982).

31. Donald C. Hambrick and Charles C. Snow, "Measuring Organizational Strategies: Some Theoretical and Methodological Problems," *Academy of Management Review,* Vol. 5, No. 4 (1980), pp. 527–38.

32. Mintzberg, "Patterns."

33. Hambrick and Snow, "Measuring Organizational Strategies."

34. Christopher Freeman, *The Economics of Industrial Innovation* (New York: Penguin, 1974).

35. William J. Abernathy and Kenneth Wayne, "Limits of the Learning Curve," in Michael Tushman and William Moore, *Readings,* pp. 109–21; and Alan M. Kantrow, "The Strategy–Technology Connection," *Harvard Business Review* (July-August 1980), pp. 6–21.

36. Day, "Strategic Perspective"; and Wind, *Product Policy.*

37. Crawford, *New Products.*

38. For a fuller discussion of formulating portfolio innovation strategies, see Judith B. Kamm, "The Portfolio Approach to Divisional Innovation Strategy," *The Journal of Business Strategy* (Summer 1986), pp. 25–36.

3

The Idea Phase of Innovation

Despite their intangibility, new ideas are an essential resource for organizations. Just as managers are responsible for procuring and maintaining other kinds of resources, such as cash, so too are they responsible for getting and keeping a ready supply of new ideas. One rule of thumb is that it takes one hundred or more ideas to obtain one or two that are good enough to consider seriously.

Like other resources, however, new ideas can be wasted. While some may certainly remain usable over a long time period, others may quickly lose their value if not used soon. Wasting new ideas can be costly in a number of ways. In addition to the cost of a lost opportunity, not using a good idea can send a message to its originator that such ideas are not desired or rewarded. Even if the originator has other ideas in the future, he or she may be reluctant to contribute them. Therefore, a cost of not using good new ideas when they are current may be more difficulty in eliciting them in the future.

Although much of the time it may be difficult to get enough usable new ideas, it is possible that managers of organizations that are consolidating, stabilizing, or divesting may not need new ideas except to solve the problems posed by these particular activities. Too many new ideas that have potential but cannot be used successfully at the time proposed may actually become destructive, pushing the organization in directions that it is not capable of following, given its other problems. Therefore, there may be times in an organization's existence when managers should work to reduce the amount of creativity or to direct it toward solving very specific problems without damaging its sources for future use.

Thus, innovation and solving problems in new ways are very closely related. A better understanding of under what conditions and from where new ideas come should enable managers to more effectively set a climate that elicits, nurtures, and channels the desired level of creative problem solving in their organizations.

The Process of Getting New Ideas

The first step in innovation is invention. It is different from, but an integral part of, innovation. Invention is the discovery or creation of a new idea, whereas innovation is its adoption or use.[1] Although there is obviously a difference between getting an idea of one's own and becoming aware of someone else's idea, there are some similarities in the process of idea generation and adoption.

For instance, new ideas can be tenuous. Common metaphors for them are "just a gleam," a "glimmer," or an "inkling." There may be suggestions, hints, or clues that are partially unformed, without definite boundaries, unsolidified, and not well understood. Some seem to defy articulation and evaporate quickly. Others only take shape as they are articulated. New ideas are delicate and can be easily destroyed. Personal accounts and other research point to a progression of invention. The first step is "preparation" in which a thorough but often fruitless analysis of the problem, question, or issue is consciously performed.[2]

As figure 3–1 indicates, combining existing facts and relationships (information) into new patterns is one approach that can be accomplished either non-rationally—by sheer imagination or intuition—or rationally—by systematic search methods and analysis. This patterning is probably most common in industry because of the constraints under which companies function. It is often less expensive and time consuming to work with what the company already has.

Another method of creating and discovering new ideas is to juxtapose knowledge from one academic discipline or industry onto knowledge from an-

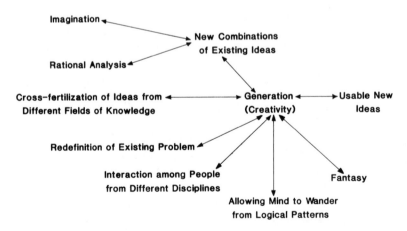

Source: From Judith B. Kamm, *How To Manage the New Product Development Process* (New York: AMACOM, 1982), p. 16. Reprinted with permission.

Figure 3–1. Processes Leading to New Ideas

other. This may be done by individuals with a broad scope of knowledge and experience or by interdisciplinary teams.

Sometimes new ideas are conceived when an existing problem is reformulated or is considered from a different point of view. This kind of "kaleidoscope" approach to problem solving can occur when a person or group unfamiliar with the issues begins work on them.[3] "Seeing with fresh eyes" can generate solutions that otherwise might not emerge. Thus, people who represent different intellectual backgrounds and perspectives (such as practicing cardiovascular specialists and theoretically oriented mechanical engineers) may stimulate each other to generate or discover ideas that have never before been considered by either individual or group.

When individuals can unleash their minds from conventional wisdom, from logical or organizational constraints, and from other forms of structure imposed upon their thinking, they may be able to develop unique concepts of solutions to existing problems. Closely related to this process is fantasizing, in which most existing conditions are ignored or modified so that individuals or groups can explore their interests in an unlimited way.

The second step is "incubation." Here, the person does not voluntarily or consciously think about the problem, but it has been hypothesized that the mind is processing the data at some unconscious level. Individuals may selectively expose themselves to new ideas congruent with their needs, attitudes, and interests. Usually, a felt need for something increases the chance that someone will become aware of a new idea that in some way satisfies that need. Needs may be thought of as conditions in which one's desires outweigh actualities.[4]

The next step is "illumination," the "instantaneous and unexpected" flash or click of a fully developed idea or solution occurring to the person. This stage is also involuntary. It cannot be willed; it just happens.[5] Consideration of a new idea may not pass beyond this awareness stage if it does not appear to be useful to the individual's situation. This perception may explain why some ideas, especially solutions to particular problems, seem to spring full-formed into a person's mind.[6] It could be said that at this stage the individual is simultaneously the generator and adopter of an idea.

Stimulating Idea Generation

Little research has focussed specifically upon the earliest phase of innovation, when ideas are first generated or discovered. Much of the work on the adoption of innovations has limited itself to explaining why a fully developed innovation is adopted or not adopted.[7] Similarly, work on the conditions associated with introduction of new products tends to include the entire innovation process, or simply the rate or number of new items generated by individuals or organizations.

Nonetheless, a body of common wisdom has developed, some of which is supported by research as well as by anecdotal evidence. The evidence may not be conclusive in a scientific sense.[8] It may be helpful for managers, however, many of whom are resigned to the fact that they practice an art in which there is rarely one best way to do anything, and who are well practiced in judging for themselves the usefulness of advice.

Sources of New Ideas: Creative People

It is unrealistic to assume that all members of an organization are equally creative. Differences in individual creativity do exist. Few people are able to generate many usable ideas. Relatively few people are immediately open to new ideas. A critical question for managers of innovation, then, is: How do I know an innovative individual when I see one?

For a number of reasons this question is difficult to answer precisely. Most of the processes underlying the generation and adoption of new ideas occur inside a person's mind and cannot be directly observed. Written or spoken ideas are the only output that can be evaluated for evidence of these processes. If such output is available at all, however, it may not be a reliable indicator of a person's potential in an organization. Another difficulty is that there are few single personality or cognitive traits or personal characteristics that correlate strongly with innovative activity. Consequently, most tests or methods devised as predictors of creativity have failed.

Nonetheless, the large body of research that has been done on what makes some people very creative and how they approach problems need not be ignored altogether, as long as the conclusions are viewed as tentative. The following rough composite profile summarizes much of what is believed to be true about innovative adults.[9]

A variety of studies has led to the general conclusion that people who are likely to become aware of ideas before other people do are those with more education and higher social status.[10] The same has also been found of those who generate new ideas.[11] Early innovators (both creators and discoverers) also tend to have more exposure to such communication channels as mass media, interpersonal relationships, and contact with change agents.[12] They tend to participate in more organizations, including social groups, and their orientation is toward their professions or the broader context surrounding their lives rather than toward the particular organization in which they work or the community in which they live. In other words, people who are "cosmopolitan" rather than "local" in their interests and loyalties tend to become aware of new ideas earlier than anyone else.[13]

One dominant characteristic of creative people appears to be that their orientation is intellectual rather than emotional or physical. If a person consistently adds unique, personal analysis or conclusions to whatever is being considered, his or her orientation is intellectual. This observation does not imply that creative people are always extraordinarily intelligent. In fact, some people have extremely high IQs (as measured by intelligence tests), but do not or cannot generate many usable new ideas.

Thus, it is the nature or quality of intelligence rather than IQ score that distinguishes creative people. Their kind of intelligence permits them to change their frame of reference and their approach to problems spontaneously. They are able to get many ideas rapidly. They are also able to give unusual answers to questions, respond atypically to situations, and offer original interpretations of events.

Organizations hoping to attract and keep creative people, then, must be able to tolerate if not warmly accept their heightened individuality. Creative organizations allow eccentricity and include marginal, unusual types of people.[14] It has also been observed that the more tightly organized a research operation is and the more teamwork is emphasized, the less likely it is that such oddballs with be tolerated.[15]

Quite frequently, those who innovate are independent in their judgments and are apt to adhere to them strongly in a disagreement. They tend to persist in their beliefs and in their commitment to their own internal standards of excellence. Related to these traits of independence and persistence is the tendency of creative people to question authority. They are likely to view authority as simply conventional or arbitrary, and they may only accept it as a matter of expedience rather than as a matter of moral obligation or personal loyalty. To gain and keep creative people's acceptance of their authority, leaders must continually display their superiority in their area of expertise or responsibility.

Innovators' intellectual independence can require that organizations hoping to keep them should be prepared to give them enough autonomy and freedom so that they can set their own directions and make many of their own decisions about their work. One study comparing effective and ineffective research laboratories, for instance, found that the less-effective labs used more formal rules and procedures for coordination and control, and that professionals saw their work activities as more controlled and well defined.[16] Another study found that without exception, research directors mentioned freedom as a highly important factor in overall levels of creativity.[17]

There is such a thing, however, as too much freedom and autonomy. A good example of how some employees respond to too little information from and contact with management is found in *The Soul of a New Machine*, which documents the invention of a new computer at Data General. One alienated young engineer left the project, as did a variety of other people. Nonetheless, despite its human costs, the invention was considered to be extremely successful.[18]

In fact, some support and direction are desired by engineers, but not too much.[19] In terms of leadership style, a participative approach that builds interpersonal relationships with creative employees and includes them in making decisions about their work appears to be more effective than a laissez-faire approach.[20] Jay Lorsch and John Morse found, for example, that in high-performance labs, researchers were involved in selecting projects and setting performance parameters and milestones.[21] Such participation makes sense when one considers that creative people are most motivated to tackle a problem by their own personal interest in it for its own sake rather than because someone in a position of authority believes it is important.

Furthermore, creative people are also motivated by feedback about their performance from their managers. Innovators often have a high need for recognition[22] as well as achievement.[23] Many engineers, in particular, seem to thrive on knowing how well they are doing. While such feedback is an important managerial control mechanism because it can be used to insure that the organization's goals are being achieved, there is growing evidence that this kind of control actually stimulates rather than stifles creativity.[24]

The nature of an organization's reward system is another vital aspect of this climate. Creativity tends to be restricted when rewards are only given for tangible, practical products.[25] Additionally, it may also be stifled by rewarding those who are productive along well-established paths only.[26] Furthermore, rewards such as promotions based on anything but merit can reduce creativity.[27]

Sources of New Ideas: Information

Innovators typically look for new ideas or ideas that will lead to new ideas, both inside and outside of their organizations. The most obvious inside source is the set of existing services, products, or processes. Design, materials, and/or packaging features often serve as the root of new ideas. For generating new-product ideas, the by-products of existing products may provide clues. Not only are successful products and processes scrutinized. Rejected new-product or new-service candidates may also be reevaluated and found to offer worthwhile ideas. Product, process, and service failures and consumer complaints may have potential as well.

Sources of new ideas outside of, but in some way related to, the company include distributors, suppliers, and competitors. Technical studies, special market analyses, government reports, and newspaper, magazine and trade articles may also contain the germs of new ideas. These sources tend to provide fairly public information, and, therefore, usually do not pose legal problems concerning ownership of the idea.[28]

Another source of ideas, especially for new products, is customers. IBM gets about one-third of its new software ideas from users. Pillsbury has developed several cake mixes based upon recipes entered in its annual bake-off. In some industries, such as semiconductors and scientific instruments, it is quite common for new process machinery and instruments to be developed from users' ideas, while in others, such as plastic additives, it is not. If a manufacturer perceives the market to be too small to justify the investment in a new idea, but the user really needs it, then the user may develop the idea and make the product available until a sufficiently promising market has been created for manufacturers to move into it. If the user wants to insure itself a competitive advantage, it may also develop its own proprietary products or processes instead of buying them from a manufacturer.[29]

Despite the fact that going outside of the organization has been found to be most effective in finding new ideas and approaches,[30] outside sources of new ideas have some drawbacks. One problem is the possible resistance of in-house personnel to developing "foreign" inventions. This not-invented-here (NIH) syndrome can be spotted when remarks such as "Aren't our ideas good enough for them?" are heard.

Other outside sources of new ideas, however, may be more problematic. Among these are advertising and market research agencies, venture-capital firms, patent attorneys, retired product specialists and designers, independent outside inventors, and individual new-product and management consultants. Patents or technology developed by other companies may be licensed. Ideas from these sources may be unsolicited as well as solicited. Whatever the case, however, if the idea is used in a new product, service, or process, the company is implicitly obliged to pay the source for it.[31]

Mass communication media, such as newspapers, television, and magazines, have been found to be the most important stimulant of awareness of new products and services, with print media being the most important stimulant of awareness about new services.[32] More selective communication media (such as academic, technical, and trade publications as well as conferences, shows, and exhibitions) are other ways of conveying information that can stimulate new ideas.

Interpersonal (word-of-mouth) communication is also a supply channel for invention. Consumers in the process of adopting a new product or service are more likely to use this conduit after they have first become aware of the new market entry, turning to others who have already used it or to experts.[33] Nonetheless, there is evidence that this kind of communication is also critical in the idea-getting phase of innovation.

For example, it has been observed that engineers and applied scientists spend between 50 and 75 percent of their time communicating with others because verbal communication permits rapid information exchange, feedback, and criticism. Thus, it can be a highly efficient supply channel.[34] In fact, an association between intensive oral and written communication and innovative performance has been consistently demonstrated by research findings.[35]

Within the organization, creativity is enhanced by such ad hoc devices as interdepartmental brainstorming sessions and suggestion systems that include tangible rewards for usable new ideas.[36] Either a formal or informal system should exist to record problems, failures, complaints, and rejected proposals for innovation. In fact, top-level management's willingness to share problems and information with lower levels can be critical.[37] However, it should be noted that one of the requisites for scientific transfer is for members of several sets of subsystems to have a high degree of trust in each other and confidence in the outcome of their joint efforts.[38] Indeed, one study reported that there was unanimity among the participants that intergroup competition is unproductive conflict.[39]

A widely accepted condition for getting new ideas is the ability of creative people to communicate about aspects of their work with colleagues outside of their organization as well as inside of it. Effective scientists both seek and receive more contact with colleagues.[40] There are three kinds of information that organizational members must get from the environment: (1) what kinds of outputs the environment seeks that may require innovation in order to be more readily received by the environment, (2) discrete kinds of technology or means that may be required to produce the innovation, and (3) once the organization implements an innovation, whether the innovation is effective in meeting the demands of the environment.[41]

Other aspects of organizations that conventional wisdom claims foster new ideas are manager's willingness to hire people with liberal arts college degrees or people who explicitly consider themselves to be generalists. Also, recruiting employees representing a diversity of backgrounds, disciplines, or schools of thought permits the kind of cross-fertilization of knowledge that can produce useful new ideas. Alternatively, specialists can be rotated through a variety of different positions, requiring them to broaden their exposure to other ways of thinking. New assignments and challenges can promote innovation and increase motivation; therefore, lateral transfers can stimulate creativity.[42] Scientists should take up new specialties or projects if they have had one specific focus for several years.[43]

Experimentation and trial-and-error learning have been identified as hallmarks of the early phase of innovation. These processes are messy and unpredictable, and they can appear to waste resources. Nonetheless, managers who really want invention must be willing to be flexible and tolerant of undisciplined, disorganized, intermittent work. In fact, in less-effective laboratories, reviews and reports of work progress occurred more frequently than in effective labs in the Lorsch and Morse study.[44] When the number of research reports was used as a performance measure, widespread apathy and resignation was found. In general, monitoring too closely the work of creative people can result in their trying to look important, to get power, and to present an idea ahead of others. It therefore can cause irrational intergroup relations.[45]

Management's attitude toward creativity and its seeming chaos can play an important role in fostering or stifling it. The more receptive managers are, the more new ideas are likely to appear.[46] Furthermore, creativity is enhanced when ideas are not prejudged on rational grounds.[47] Willingness to experiment and to permit mistakes is one of the primary features of innovative companies.[48] Indeed, receptive attitudes can be displayed by not restricting organizational rewards to those who invent what turn out to be tangible, practical products, and by not rewarding only those people who are productive along well-established paths.[49]

Exploring the Conventional Wisdom about What Stimulates New Ideas

In order to determine the soundness of the preceding prescriptions, measures of individuals' innovative behavior and of their perceptions of their organizations' climate for creativity must be devised. This section describes one attempt to develop a set of such measures. It also presents the results of using them to survey scientists and engineers in the pharmaceuticals and semiconductor divisions whose innovation strategies were described in the previous chapter.

A questionnaire and cover letter from the division general manager were sent to new-product developers by in-house mail, to be returned directly to the author. The purpose of the survey was to discover whether relationships existed between new-product developers' innovativeness and their views of how their divisions managed innovation. Because of the exploratory nature of this study, however, statistical significance testing was not done. The results discussed here should therefore be interpreted as preliminary and in need of refinement and testing.

Three variables to measure innovative behavior were created from the questionnaire items about idea generation. In order to take into consideration the respondents' job tenure, the number of significant new ideas generated while in the current job was divided by the number of months spent in it. The new-product idea ratio resulted. New ideas actually used for new products divided by current job tenure became the idea-acceptance ratio. The ratio of ideas actually used to the number of ideas generated became the idea-use ratio. Table 3–1 presents not only a definition of each variable, but also the divisions' mean scores and range on each of them.

To further elaborate the meaning of these variables, table 3–1 shows that in the semiconductor industry, as represented in the sample of three firms in this book, the average output of new ideas was half as many ideas as the number of months an engineer had spent on the job (.52). In the ethical pharmaceuticals industry, on the other hand, the average was to have twice as many ideas as the number of months one had been in one's current position (2.04). Semiconductor company B had a significantly higher average new-product idea ratio than its industry counterparts, and company G's average stands out in the pharmaceuticals industry.

As the idea-use ratio scores reveal, however, fewer ideas were actually used in the pharmaceuticals industry than in the semiconductor industry. The former

Table 3-1
Divisions' Mean Scores and Industry Means for Idea-Generation, Idea-Use, and Idea-Acceptance Ratios
(raw scores prior to being bracketed)

	Semiconductor Industry				Pharmaceutical Industry				
	Co. A	Co. B	Co. C	Industry Mean	Co. D	Co. E	Co. F	Co. G	Industry Mean
Number of respondents (n) =	28	22	17		15	8	24	24	
New-product idea ratio = Number of new-product ideas ÷ Number of months in job	.40	.85	.31	.52	.32	.45	.29	7.09	2.04
Company range:	0–3.13	.03–5.00	0–1.75		.04–1.47	.04–2.50	0–4.17	0–11.25	
Idea-acceptance ratio = Number of ideas used ÷ Number of months in job	.13	.51	.22	.29	.06	.31	.07	.03	.12
Company range:	0–.62	0–3.33	0–1.75		0–.23	0–2.50	0–.66	0–.25	
Idea-use ratio = Number of ideas used ÷ Number of new product ideas	.48	.63	.46	.52	.28	.50	.33	.18	.32
Company range:	0–1.0	0–1.0	0–1.0		0–.80	0–1.00	0–1.00	0–.75	

used approximately a third whereas the latter used about half. It is particularly striking that company G only used 18 percent of the new ideas generated. As chapter two pointed out, this division's innovation strategy called for a shift to more radically new products, after having been termed a "dowager" in its industry. That is, it had a reputation of being a mature, slow-to-change organization. Reasons for difficulty in making this shift may be that management was slow to loosen the screen for accepting new ideas to explore, that a large number of poor ideas were being generated, or both. Semiconductor company B, on the other hand, with its innovation strategy successfully shifting to more revolutionary innovation, had an average acceptance ratio of .63, the highest in the entire sample. Pharmaceuticals company E, which was also trying to generate a breakthrough drug, had the second highest acceptance rate, .50.

The idea-acceptance ratio sharpens the contrast between industries, with the semiconductor industry using about a third as many ideas as the number of months the new-product developer had spent on his or her job, while the pharmaceuticals industry used only slightly over a tenth as many ideas as the length of job tenure in months. Some of this discrepancy can be explained by the fact that the product life cycle of semiconductors is usually two years or less, while that of prescription drugs is usually at least seventeen years. Therefore, the pace of innovation is slower in the drug industry, and it tends to rely more upon revolutions than in the semiconductor industry, which innovates rapidly and incrementally. The pharmaceuticals industry introduces fewer new products than does the semiconductor industry. In addition, in this sample, the average job tenure of semiconductor engineers was two years, whereas that for pharmaceuticals scientists was more than five years.

Because of the large number and wide range of values for each of the new-idea variables, their distributions were grouped into brackets to simplify interpretation. The meanings of the brackets are based on the distribution obtained from this sample, rather than on some absolute standard of what constitutes a high or low level of output. Further, the brackets do not divide the distribution into five equal parts. It was heavily skewed toward no innovative output at all. This finding supports those of other studies, which have noted that in most organizations, a fairly small coterie of people have a disproportionate number of ideas and other indications of innovative behavior.[50] Table 3–2 contains the meanings of each level of each of the three variables. In their bracketed form, the innovative behavior variables were correlated with twenty different items measuring the perceived climate for innovation in the respondents' divisions. Each of these measures was derived from other researchers' findings as cited in the previous section of this chapter. Table 3–3 presents the questionnaire item, the variable name, and the meaning of each variable's five values.

The average scores of each of the seven divisions on each of the twenty items as well as the industry average appear in table 3–4. On almost half of these measures of perceived climate for creativity, there was a great deal of similarity

Table 3–2
Bracket Levels for the Idea-Generation, Idea-Use,
and Idea-Acceptance Ratios

Variables	Bracket Levels
New-product idea ratio: $$\frac{\text{significant ideas for new products}}{\text{number of months in current job}}$$	1 = no innovative output at all 2 = average rate of less than three per year in current position 3 = average rate of between three and six per year 4 = average rate of between seven and a dozen per year 5 = average rate of more than a dozen per year
Idea-acceptance ratio: $$\frac{\text{ideas actually used}}{\text{number of months in current job}}$$	1 = no innovative output 2 = less than three per year 3 = between three and six per year 4 = between seven and a dozen per year 5 = more than a dozen per year
Idea-use ratio: $$\frac{\text{ideas actually used}}{\text{significant ideas for new products}}$$	1 = no ideas used 2 = less than 15 percent of ideas used 3 = 15 to 25 percent used 4 = between 25 and 50 percent used 5 = more than half used

across the entire sample. The majority of respondents in all seven divisions perceived that highly unusual ideas were well received by their supervisors and that most of their ideas were not too advanced to be understood and accepted by their companies' management. They also felt that their supervisors did not criticize their new ideas too much before they had really developed them.

Furthermore, most respondents perceived that producing tangible results was very important in their divisions and that their job was to turn out as many successful new products as possible. They also perceived that they were expected to work very closely with colleagues in their departments. Finally, very few new-product developers believed that competition among projects for funds made their colleagues too reluctant to share data about their work with them. It appears, then, that the management of the divisions participating in this analysis was, in fact, heeding many of the prescriptions of previous empirical findings on what conditions are most conducive to generating new ideas.

There were several differences among these divisions, however, some of which might be expected given the differences in the nature of the industries. For example, in the semiconductor industry, which generally has lower profit margins and a faster pace of more evolutionary innovation, engineers tended to perceive that it was difficult to obtain formal approval and funding for radically new ideas and that they were under pressure from management to meet dead-lines. They were also more likely to perceive that they were evaluated on the basis of how accurate their new-product estimates turned out to be once their products were introduced to the market. Furthermore, many of these engineers felt that if they needed more money to change direction on a new product, it was not easy for them to get it. These perceptions were less common among pharmaceuticals scientists.

In the pharmaceutical industry, respondents were more likely to perceive that written justification for pursuing new ideas was important in their divisions. In the semiconductor industry, there often was no time to write anything. Pharmaceuticals scientists were also more likely to feel that they were not free to discuss their work on new products with colleagues both inside and outside of their firms.

Interestingly, the measure of perceived climate for creativity labelled "Information freedom" on the correlation matrix in table 3–5 was one of the few that was related to any of the innovation measures. As predicted by previous studies, the negative relationships of .22 with the idea-use ratio and .27 with the idea-acceptance ratio indicate that respondents who had had fewer of their new ideas actually used were those who tended to perceive that they were not free to discuss their work on new products with colleagues both inside and outside of their firms.

Although affiliation with the drug industry may explain some of this relationship, if it were not also present to some extent among semiconductor respondents, or if the opposite relationship were true in that subsample, then no relationship at all would have shown up in the entire sample correlation matrix. Ideas are usually accepted if they are deemed to be useful, and information from a variety of sources both inside and outside of the organization is necessary to insure that an idea will be useful from its conception.

Other aspects of the perceived climate for creativity worth further investigation are new-product developers' ability to choose their own projects, management's receptivity to new ideas, and evaluation on the basis of accurate estimates of a new product's market performance.

As table 3–5 indicates, when respondents perceived that they were not able to choose the new-product projects on which they worked, they tended to have generated fewer significant new ideas during their job tenure ($r = -.31$). This relationship seems to support research findings cited previously in this chapter that when creative people are permitted to work on what interests them rather than on what management believes is the best use of their talent and training, then they are more likely to generate new ideas that are useful. The idea-use ratio is also associated with the ability to choose projects ($r = -.21$).

Not surprisingly, respondents who had had fewer of their ideas actually used for new products tended to perceive that most of their ideas were too advanced

Table 3–3
Perceived Climate for Innovation

Questionnaire Item	Variable Name	Meaning of the Variable's Values				
		1	2	3	4	5
1. Highly unusual ideas are well received by my supervisor.	Supervisor's receptivity	Strongly agree	Agree	Undecided	Disagree	Strongly disagree
2. Most of my ideas are too advanced to be understood and accepted by this company's management.	Management's receptivity	Strongly disagree	Disagree	Undecided	Agree	Strongly agree
3. It is difficult to obtain formal approval and funding for radically new ideas.	Funding difficulty	Strongly disagree	Disagree	Undecided	Agree	Strongly agree
4. We are rewarded too much on the basis of our ideas' practicality and not enough on how innovative they are.	Reward by practicality	Strongly disagree	Disagree	Undecided	Agree	Strongly agree
5. My supervisor criticizes my new ideas too much before I have really developed them.	Early criticism	Strongly disagree	Disagree	Undecided	Agree	Strongly agree
6. Written justification for new ideas is not important here.	Written justification	Strongly disagree	Agree	Undecided	Disagree	Strongly agree
7. Writing progress reports takes too much of my time.	Progress reports	Strongly disagree	Disagree	Undecided	Agree	Strongly agree
8. I am not under pressure from management to meet deadlines.	Deadline pressure	Strongly disagree	Agree	Undecided	Disagree	Strongly disagree
9. Producing tangible results is not very important here.	Tangible results	Strongly agree	Agree	Undecided	Disagree	Strongly disagree
10. I am evaluated on the basis of how accurate my new-product estimates turn out to be once my product is introduced to the market.	Accuracy estimates	Strongly disagree	Disagree	Undecided	Agree	Strongly agree

11.	I am not expected to work very closely with colleagues in my department.	Teamwork	Strongly agree	Agree	Undecided	Disagree	Strongly disagree
12.	There are too many oddballs and not enough teamplayers here.	Oddballs	Strongly agree	Agree	Undecided	Disagree	Strongly disagree
13.	I am able to choose the new-product projects on which I work.	Choose projects	Strongly agree	Agree	Undecided	Disagree	Strongly disagree
14.	If I need more money to change direction on a new product, it is easy for me to get it.	Availability of funds	Strongly agree	Agree	Undecided	Disagree	Strongly disagree
15.	My job prevents me from branching out into new areas of knowledge or technical skills.	Scope of job	Strongly disagree	Disagree	Undecided	Agree	Strongly agree
16.	My job is to turn out as many successful new products as possible.	Importance of output	Strongly disagree	Disagree	Undecided	Agree	Strongly agree
17.	It should be easier for me to get information that I need to develop my ideas from other departments in this company.	Information access	Strongly disagree	Disagree	Undecided	Agree	Strongly agree
18.	I am free to discuss my work on new products with colleagues both inside and outside the firm.	Information freedom	Strongly agree	Agree	Undecided	Disagree	Strongly disagree
19.	My supervisor does not provide me with enough information about how I am doing or how my ideas are received.	Feedback	Strongly agree	Agree	Undecided	Disagree	Strongly disagree
20.	Competition among projects for funds makes my colleagues too reluctant to share data about their work with me.	Competition block	Strongly disagree	Disagree	Undecided	Agree	Strongly agree

Table 3–4
Average Perceived Climate for Innovation Measures in Each Division and Industry

Measures	Co. A (n = 51[a])	Co. B (n = 30)	Co. C (n = 26)	Semiconductor Industry Average	Co. D (n = 21)	Co. E (n = 18)	Co. F (n = 40)	Co. G (n = 32)	Pharmaceuticals Industry Average
Supervisor's receptivity	2.76	2.27	2.65	2.56	2.52	2.17	2.45	2.88	2.51
Management's receptivity	2.28	2.20	2.42	2.30	1.85	1.89	2.03	2.09	1.97
Funding difficulty	3.70	3.67	3.62	3.66	2.81	2.67	3.25	3.47	3.05
Reward by practicality	3.08	3.00	2.72	2.93	2.67	2.71	2.93	3.27	2.90
Early criticism	2.31	1.97	2.35	2.21	2.29	1.89	2.35	2.56	2.27
Written justification	3.28	3.30	3.44	3.34	2.67	3.61	3.70	4.19	3.54
Progress reports	2.51	2.50	2.35	2.45	2.76	3.06	3.03	2.41	2.82
Deadline pressure	3.65	3.80	4.00	3.82	2.91	3.39	3.95	3.00	3.31
Tangible results	4.41	4.40	4.42	4.41	4.24	4.00	4.38	4.34	4.24
Accuracy of estimates	3.10	2.93	3.44	3.16	1.95	2.50	2.62	2.27	2.34
Teamwork	3.90	3.93	4.07	3.97	4.05	4.39	3.90	3.67	4.00
Oddballs	3.39	3.97	3.08	3.48	3.57	3.67	3.65	3.44	3.58
Choose projects	3.26	2.97	3.42	3.22	2.14	2.77	3.83	3.41	3.04

Availability of funds	3.61	3.47	3.68	3.59	2.86	2.56	3.30	3.04	2.94
Scope of job	2.75	2.60	2.89	2.75	2.05	2.22	2.56	2.61	2.36
Importance of output	3.69	3.60	4.04	3.78	3.71	3.71	3.51	4.19	3.78
Information access	3.67	3.58	3.58	3.61	2.52	2.94	3.23	3.50	3.05
Information freedom	3.61	3.03	2.85	3.16	3.57	3.47	3.98	4.42	3.86
Feedback	2.86	3.50	2.62	2.99	3.52	3.41	3.18	2.97	3.27
Competition block	2.24	2.30	2.42	2.32	2.05	1.81	2.59	2.23	2.17

[a]n = number of respondents.

Table 3–5
Correlations of Ideas versus Perceived Creativity Climate Measures
(number of respondents = 218)

	New Product Idea	Idea Acceptance	Idea Use		New Product Idea	Idea Acceptance	Idea Use
New Product Idea	1.00			Tangible results	−.02	.02	.13
Idea Acceptance	.22	1.00		Accuracy of estimates	.14	.16	.35
Idea Use	.75	.58	1.00	Teamwork	.01	.06	.05
Supervisor's receptivity	−.09	−.11	−.09	Oddballs	.12	.09	.07
Management's receptivity	−.03	−.20	−.13	Choose projects	−.31	−.07	−.21
Funding difficulty	.08	.03	.16	Availability of funds	−.03	.10	.06
Reward by practicality	.06	.04	.03	Scope of job	−.04	.05	.02
Early criticism	−.16	−.13	−.08	Importance of output	.13	.08	.13
Written justification	−.04	−.12	−.18	Information access	.01	.08	.10
Progress Reports	.13	.07	.14	Information freedom	−.06	−.27	−.22
				Feedback	.09	.04	.01
Deadline pressure	−.07	−.06	.05	Competition block	−.02	−.04	.11

to be understood and accepted by their company's management. The correlation coefficient between the idea-acceptance ratio and management's receptivity was −.20.

With the exception of these few moderately strong relationships, however, table 3–5 suggests that many other aspects of perceived climate for creativity had little bearing on idea generation or use. While many of the coefficients' signs are negative, as hypothesized by previous research, there are some notable exceptions. For example, respondents' perceptions that it was difficult to obtain formal approval and funding for radically new ideas, that they were rewarded too much on the basis of their ideas' practicality and not enough on how innovative they were, and that writing progress reports took too much of their time did not necessarily mean that they tended to generate fewer ideas and get them used.

Those measures that were almost constant across the sample, such as the perceived importance of teamwork and producing tangible results, do not explain why companies B and E stand out in having the highest average scores on measures of idea generation and use. It may be that the innovation strategies in these divisions (perceptions of which were not studied in this survey) may be more important in understanding the early stages of innovation than are the perceived climates for creativity.

The results of exploring the conventional wisdom about the best ways to stimulate inventiveness or the generation of usable new ideas, then, show that there are few strong relationships between these measures and actual output of ideas. It is therefore difficult to conclude that if a manager follows all the well-known prescriptions, greater innovativeness will automatically take place. It may well be that satisfying the conditions described in this chapter are necessary but not sufficient for a high level of idea generation or discovery. In other words, in order to stimulate and maintain any inventiveness at all, these conditions probably should exist, as they do in most of the seven companies studied. These conditions or climates for creativity alone, however, will not guarantee that a great number of ideas will be generated or discovered.

Managing the earliest phase of innovation, when new ideas are formed, may require the most delicate balancing act of any of the phases of this process. On the one hand, managers should use enough of their power to insure that creative people have a sense of direction and the resources they need in order to get new ideas. On the other hand, managers should basically let these people make most of the decisions about the task of invention.

Managers should be receptive to new ideas and supportive without making judgments or giving the impression that their advice is to be taken as an order. Their relationships with creative people should be the most important source of influence at this phase. Otherwise, it is at this point that "they who manage least manage best." Thus, managers play a relatively passive, behind-the-scenes role. As new ideas develop and the successive phases of innovation occur, there is increasing need for active management. The next chapter describes the feasibility assessment phase in which managers play a slightly larger part.

Notes

1. Everett M. Rogers, *Diffusion of Innovations*, 3rd ed. (New York: Free Press, 1983).

2. Albert Rothenberg and Carl R. Hausman (eds.), *The Creativity Question* (Durham, N.C.: Duke University Press, 1976).

3. Rosabeth Moss Kanter, *The Change Masters: Innovation for Productivity in the American Corporation* (New York: Simon and Schuster, 1983).

4. Rogers, *Diffusion*.

5. Rothenberg and Hausman, *Creativity Question*, pp. 63–79.

6. Rogers, *Diffusion*.

7. Lawrence B. Mohr, *Explaining Organizational Behavior* (San Francisco: Jossey-Bass, 1982).

8. Everett M. Rogers and J.D. Eveland, "Communication and Innovation in Orga-

nizations," in P. Kelly and M. Kransberg (eds.), *Technological Innovation: A Critical Review of Current Knowledge*, Vol. II (San Francisco: San Francisco University Press, 1978); G.W. Downs and Lawrence B. Mohr, "Conceptual Issues in the Study of Innovation," *Administrative Science Quarterly*, Vol. 21 (1976), pp. 700–14; and W.J. Bigoness and W.D. Perreault, "A Conceptual Paradigm and Approach for the Study of Innovators," *Academy of Management Journal*, Vol. 24, No. 1 (1981), pp. 68–82.

9. Unless specifically attributed to other sources, the profile of creative people is drawn from the following: Gary A. Steiner, *The Creative Organization* (Chicago: University of Chicago Press, 1965); Rothenberg and Hausman, *Creativity Question*; C. Merle Crawford, *New Products Management* (Homewood, Ill.: Richard D. Irwin, 1983); and Rogers, *Diffusion*.

10. Everett M. Rogers with Floyd F. Shoemaker, *Communication of Innovations: A Cross-Cultural Approach* (New York: Free Press, 1971).

11. Robert T. Keller and Winford E. Holland, "Communicators and Innovators in Research and Development Organizations," *Academy of Management Journal*, Vol. 26, No. 4 (1983), pp. 742–49.

12. Rogers, *Diffusion*; and Keller and Holland, "Communicators and Innovators."

13. Thomas S. Robertson and Yoram Wind, "Organizational Cosmopolitanism and Innovativeness," *Academy of Management Journal*, Vol. 26, No. 2 (1983), pp. 332–38.

14. Steiner, *Creative Organization*, p. 16.

15. Norman Kaplan, "Some Organizational Factors Affecting Creativity," in Charles D. Orth, III, Joseph C. Bailey, and Francis W. Wolek (eds.), *Administering Research and Development* (Homewood, Ill.: Richard D. Irwin, 1964).

16. Jay W. Lorsch and John J. Morse, *Organizations and Their Members: A Contingency Approach* (New York: Harper & Row, 1974).

17. Kaplan, "Factors."

18. Tracy Kidder, *The Soul of a New Machine* (Boston: Atlantic-Little, Brown, 1981).

19. Leonard Sayles, "Case Studies of Three Companies: Barriers to Innovation," in Orth, Bailey, and Wolek, *Administering Research*, p. 420.

20. Paul Hersey and Kenneth Blanchard, *Management of Organizational Behavior: Utilizing Human Resources*, 4th ed. (Englewood Cliffs, N.J.: Prentice-Hall, 1982).

21. Lorsch and Morse, *Organizations*, pp. 100–1.

22. Michael Kirton, "Adaptors and Innovators: A Description and Measure," *Journal of Applied Psychology*, Vol. 61, No. 5 (1976), pp. 622–29.

23. Augustus Abbey and John W. Dickson, "R&D Work Climate and Innovation in Semiconductors," *Academy of Management Journal*, Vol. 26, No. 2 (1983), pp. 362–68.

24. "Creativity by the Numbers: An Interview with Robert Noyce," *Harvard Business Review* (May-June 1980), pp. 122–32.

25. Kaplan, "Factors," p. 109.

26. Donald C. Pelz and Frank M. Andrews, *Scientists in Organizations: Productive Climates for Research and Development* (New York: John Wiley & Sons, 1966), p. 173.

27. Steiner, *Creative Organization*; and Abbey and Dickson, "R&D Work Climate."

28. E. Patrick McGuire, *Generating New-Product Ideas* (New York: Conference Board, 1972).

29. Eric A. von Hippel, "Users as Innovators," in *Innovation or How to Make New Things Happen*, prepared by the editors of *Technology Review* (Cambridge, Mass.: Massachusetts Institute of Technology, Technology Review, 1984).

30. James M. Utterback, "The Process of Innovation: A Study of the Origination and Development of Ideas for New Scientific Instruments," *IEEE Transactions on Engineering Management* (EM–18), pp. 124–31.

31. McGuire, *Generating*, p. 53.

32. James F. Engel and Roger D. Blackwell, *Consumer Behavior*, 4th ed. (New York: Dryden, 1982).

33. Ibid., p. 397.

34. Richard S. Rosenbloom and Francis W. Wolek, *Technology, Information, and Organization: Information Transfer in Industrial R&D* (Boston: Harvard University Graduate School of Business Administration, 1967).

35. Michael L. Tushman, "Managing Communication Networks in R&D Laboratories," in Michael L. Tushman and William L. Moore (eds.), *Readings in the Management of Innovation* (Boston: Pitman, 1982); and Michael L. Tushman and Thomas J. Scanlan, "Boundary Spanning Individuals: Their Role in Information Transfer and Their Antecedents," *Academy of Management Journal*, Vol. 2 (1981), pp. 289–305.

36. Steiner, *Creative Organization*, p. 16; and George S. Prince, *The Practice of Creativity* (New York: Collier, 1970).

37. Kanter, *Change Masters*.

38. Jay W. Lorsch, *Product Innovation and Organization* (New York: Macmillan, 1965).

39. Sayles, "Case Studies," p. 408.

40. Pelz and Andrews, *Scientists*, p. 35.

41. Gerald Zaltman, Robert Duncan, and Jonny Holbek, *Innovations and Organizations* (New York: John Wiley & Sons, 1973).

42. Paul H. Thompson and Gene W. Dalton, "Are R&D Organizations Obsolete?" *Harvard Business Review* (November-December 1976), pp. 105–16.

43. Pelz and Andrews, *Scientists*, p. 173.

44. Lorsch and Morse, *Organizations*, p. 88.

45. Sayles, "Case Studies," p. 421–22.

46. Kaplan, "Factors," pp. 101–3.

47. Steiner, *Creative Organization*, p. 16; and Prince, *Practice*, 1970.

48. Thomas J. Peters and Robert H. Waterman, Jr., *In Search of Excellence* (New York: Harper & Row, 1982).

49. Kaplan, "Factors," p. 109; and Pelz and Andrews, *Scientists*, p. 173.

50. Keller and Holland, "Communicators and Innovators," 1983.

4

Reality-Testing

Not all new ideas are good ones. In considering innovation, the word *good* means, among other things, valid and practical. There is a wide variety of reasons why many ideas cannot be used. The materials needed to put the idea into tangible form may not exist or may be too rare and costly. Not enough people may have the needed expertise to develop or use the idea. There may not be enough financial and/or human resources in the organization to take the idea any further. Whatever the reason, ideas that cannot meet the needs of an organization's members and their markets or clients generally remain just ideas.

In the previous chapter, the generation of new ideas was described in three stages: preparation, incubation, and illumination. The fourth stage is "verification." During this stage, the new idea is tested for validity, and it is consciously refined so that it can be used.[1] Thus, logical reasoning and information are applied to intuition in order to fit the idea to reality.

Therefore, after an individual or group generates or discovers an idea, the first decision that must be made is whether or not to pursue it further. The reality-testing phase for some new ideas may be very cursory under certain circumstances. Such is the case in highly formalized organizations in which explicit goals and criteria have been preset and new ideas are designed to conform to them.[2] General management has designed the system or established the constraints. The innovators know the idea is feasible because its very nature is to solve a problem posed by a set of limits or constraints.

In many other instances, however, the invention phase is not so structured, and early reality-testing represents the first attempt at any kind of evaluation of a new idea. It can be a fairly long process, requiring the idea's originator to seek help from more people in the organization.

Most models of new-product development include a feasibility assessment phase early in the process.[3] Likewise, the best- known model of innovation adoption includes the "persuasion stage" as its second step.[4] Persuasion is defined as the potential adopter's formation of an attitude about a new idea that can color his or her actions. In this stage, the potential adopter actively seeks more information about the new idea. Information gathering also begins in the feasibility assessment phase of idea generation, as the developer tries to learn whether or not the product can be made, the service can be offered, or the organizational form can be established.

The important behaviors in this stage are where information is sought, what messages are received, and how they are interpreted. The ability to think "hypothetically and counter-factually and to project into the future" is as important at this stage of idea generation as at the persuasion stage of adoption.[5] Reality-testing, then, is not a completely objective, factual activity. It may be based purely on abstract reasoning.

In both kinds of innovation, reality-testing is an attempt to reduce uncertainty by getting more information about the idea's requirements and consequences. Gathering data, however, can take a lot of time—a precious resource. Delays in introducing a new product or service or in implementing a new process technology can diminish their chances for success. Thus, there are costs as well as benefits involved in evaluating new ideas in their early phase.

These costs and benefits should be carefully weighed by general managers who design innovation evaluation procedures. Such procedures represent management's attempt to influence innovators' decisions about new ideas, and they include such requirements as how much and what kind of information is needed to determine feasibility. What is required to prove feasibility can become a kind of screen that if too fine can miss potential breakthroughs and if too coarse can waste time and money on useless ideas.

It should be noted, however, that determining whether or not a new idea is feasible is different from determining whether or not it should be further developed. Deciding upon desirability is a later phase of managing innovation and will be discussed in a subsequent chapter.

Innovation failures cost real time and money as opposed to the cost of lost opportunities, which are more difficult to quantify and are not as apparent to investors. Therefore, most textbooks on product development (idea generation) and capital budgeting (idea adoption) imply that it is better to err on the side of conservatism.[6] They tend to suggest that firms should evaluate all new ideas with the same fine screen.

Empirical research testing these prescriptions, however, is rare. In general, aside from the marketing literature on concept testing, little has been written specifically about this phase of innovation in business organizations.

Determining the Need to Check Reality

The Type of Innovation

For certain types of innovation there is very little, if any, question about whether or not it is possible to develop the new idea further. Two dimensions of the typology in table 1–1 are critical in determining how much of the reality-testing phase of the innovation process should be undertaken. The first is what has been termed the "extent" dimension of a new idea—its degree of difference from what already exists. It is logical to assume that if a new idea is similar in many ways to that which already exists, then only the different feature(s) need to be investigated to learn whether or not it is feasible.

For example, if a department store's executives discover the idea of adding a career-wardrobe–planning service to their business, then the only feasibility-testing that they might need to do is to determine whether their store carries the kind of clothing suitable to whatever careers they envision. Such a reality check can be done almost instantaneously because presumably they know what lines of merchandise they carry. This innovation is not very different from the kind of service that some dedicated salespeople may be providing informally, free of charge.

On the other hand, if this same group of executives came up with the idea of offering executive travel planning and reservations in an executive "boutique" featuring wardrobe planning as well, then more effort to check feasibility would be needed. Travel service is quite different from clothing service.

The second dimension of innovation is its timing. If the innovator is the third or later of its referent group to develop or adopt a new idea, then the pioneering innovator and the immediate successor have already proven its feasibility, at least for their organizations. It must be remembered that feasibility here is not considered to be objective. It depends upon the limits within which the new idea exists. If the late following organization is similar to its predecessors, then an idea's feasibility is quite likely.

If a large company's human resource director learns about computer-based career planning by reading an article in the trade press about how it is done by a large competitor, it is reasonable to assume that a similar innovation could be adopted by his or her company. If the owner of a small firm reads the same article, however, more reality-testing would be necessary.

The Organization's Strategy

When innovators within an organizational context get ideas for doing new things or for doing the same things in new ways, they also are potentially changing the organization's strategy. In chapter 2, strategy was defined as a pattern of decisions about organizational objectives and plans for achieving them. In the above example of the department store executives who developed the concept of offering executive travel as well as wardrobe-planning services, this innovation could expand the nature of the business in which this department store engages. If a scientist in a pharmaceuticals firm specializing in human health care discovers a chemical compound that prevents the reproduction of certain kinds of insects harmful to food crops, then this invention could change significantly the markets to which it sells its products.

Because of new ideas' potential to influence organizational strategy, it is important to consider strategy in determining the need for reality-testing. This, of course, assumes that innovators know what their organization's strategy is. If the new idea falls well within the organization's definition of what it is and wants to be, then reality-testing may be less necessary than it would be if the new idea falls near or outside of the organization's boundary of activities. If the invention fits with existing strategy, then the necessary human expertise, the physical facilities and equipment, and the market are more likely to exist, thereby making further development of it feasible.

When new ideas represent important shifts from the way in which the organization currently operates, the first question that innovators should ask is, how flexible is top management about the organization's strategy? In other words, how likely is it to consider changing it in some way to accommodate this innovation? If it is clear that the strategy is rigid, then the ill-fitting new idea is probably not feasible in that particular organization. There are many possible reasons why management might resist shifting its strategy, including a high degree of success or a recently completed strategy formulation or reformulation.

If it is not clear that the strategy is rigid, however, then reality-testing along this dimension, as well as others to be described in the next section, becomes necessary. Innovators should sound out their superiors to learn their general openness to new opportunities beyond what the organization is currently doing. In addition, knowledge about top management's interests can help innovators to predict in which direction(s) it might be willing to move. Such information can be gathered quite informally, without referring to specific new ideas.

Another aspect of organizational strategy that is useful to consider in determining the need to check the feasibility of a new idea is that of the organization's uniqueness. In other words, how different is the organization from its competitors or counterparts, and in what ways does it differ? Knowledge of uniqueness permits an innovator to know whether or not a new idea's feasibility can be tested simply by examining other organizations' experience with it.

The Innovation's Environmental Impact

In industries regulated by government agencies (especially agencies responsible for societal health and safety), ideas for new products and technological processes cannot be considered feasible if they do not conform to the appropriate standards. Early in the new idea's evolution, therefore, they should be used as screening criteria.

In general, then, there are six conditions under any one of which reality-testing should be included as part of the innovation process. These conditions are: (1) when the new idea is very different from that which exists, (2) when the innovator is among the first to get the idea, (3) when the idea does not fit with the organization's existing strategy, (4) when the organization's strategic flexibility is unknown, (5) when the organization is very different from its competitors and counterparts, and (6) when the innovation will be subject to externally imposed regulations.

Reality-Testing in Two High Technology Industries

Many textbooks tell—and organizations' managements expect—innovators to document a new concept's feasibility with predetermined kinds of information gathered and presented in specified ways. In other words, before any idea can move beyond its conceptualization phase in many organizations, there must be proof that it can be developed further into a reality. This requirement applies as much to the adoption of, say, new processing equipment as it does to the generation of a new service.

In general, there is a great deal of similarity among the three semiconductor and four pharmaceuticals divisions' approach to reality-testing despite significant differences between the two industries. For example, all of them most of the time, if not always, check out new ideas with in-house sales and/or production people or with prospective customers before prototypes (the first physical manifestation of the new thing) are made. Furthermore, not only are ideas reality-tested in their idea format, but the first prototypes are also tested. Because the cost of preparing a prototype can be fairly high in some industries, enough preliminary feasibility-testing must occur even before this more concrete step can be taken. In the ethical pharmaceuticals industry, for instance, the four companies studied here included a "prefeasibility" phase in their formal product-development cycles.

The Pharmaceuticals Industry

In company D, research management has the opportunity to be influential in screening new drug compounds before they undergo feasibility-testing because the executive directors of the various research groups are free to attend research committee and project team meetings. The prototype is the first batch of the compound that is prepared for use in preclinical testing, and research committees are responsible for evaluating the results of these tests.

Project teams report to either of two therapeutics group managers in company E. The group managers screen new-product ideas before they undergo feasibility-testing. One manager noted that a researcher may see an article of interest, clip it, and send it to him. He feels it is best to discourage early on an idea that is too far out, rather than to wait for a year, after the person has invested time and effort in it. This prefeasibility phase is known as "pre-phase I" at company E. A diagram of its appears in figure 4–1. About 60 percent of the compounds considered are rejected at this stage.

The vice president of R&D at company F generally delegates the screening

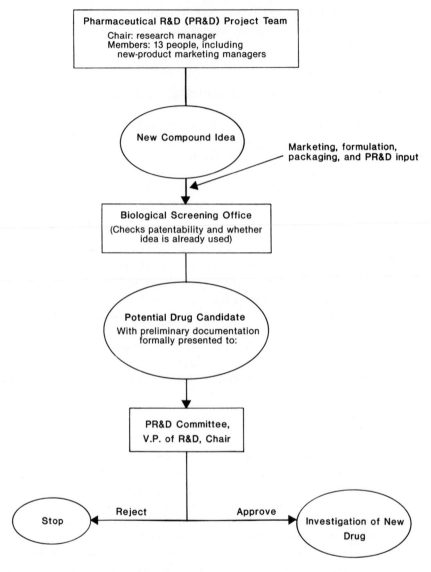

Note: Average duration: six months to one year. Drug compound made in bulk by PR&D staff.

Figure 4–1. The Reality-Testing Phase in Pharmaceutical Company E

of new-product ideas to specialists in the R&D unit. Most ideas from outside of the company are given to physicians in the development department, who immediately send an agreement form to the person or group making the suggestion in order to protect company F from future lawsuits. They then screen for ideas' legal and regulatory implications. If an idea has merit, scientists and other experts are called together to form a team to evaluate it further.

The vice president himself screens ideas coming from academic institutions. If they are worthy of pursuit, he passes them down to the most knowledgeable people for their opinions. In rare cases, such as recombinant DNA, he reserves judgment for himself. He "captured" the DNA idea and "quietly engaged" others' interest in it, sending it to an offshore facility for preliminary work. The larger and more important an idea seems to be, the greater the vice president's role in it, and the less the likelihood that he will delegate it.

Known as the "create" and "preprove" phases at company F, the prefeasibility phase consists primarily of laboratory experiments in animals. Many of the tests are routine; among the major tasks are scheduling and monitoring the tests, and getting supplies made. Consequently, the research department figures most prominently at this stage, as well as at the "research mission" stage later.

Marketing input used to be sought in the form of a five-year discounted cash flow analysis, but this practice was found to be impossible and is no longer required. Instead, marketing people are asked, "What do you need to know so that you can make good decisions?" and they are given an early product profile. They can then make suggestions to R&D. As one manager noted, "No one's career is on the line at this point."

Approximately 25 percent of new ideas are rejected by the end of this stage. They are filtered with the assumption that it is acceptable for researchers to work on them for a while, but the central question is, "Do they have great potential in the market?" If their potential is judged to be only modest, the project is usually dropped.

The vice president of product development in company G, called the Research Institute, screens new-product ideas before they undergo feasibility-testing. Project teams submit "technical service requests," which his department must sign before development can continue. The Institute's president, a biologist, also screens new ideas. An average of 60 percent of ideas are rejected before the prototype is made. If new ideas are feasible, they are labelled "investigational new drugs," and are filed with the U.S. Food and Drug Administration. Twenty percent of new compounds are rejected after the prototype has been made and tested.

The Semiconductor Industry

Despite the fact that new semiconductors are quite different entities from new pharmaceuticals, they too undergo at least a brief prefeasibility phase of development in all three of the companies in this sample. Semiconductor company B's approach to new ideas is the most informal. The vice president of strategic operations (to whom the codirectors of the Applied Research and Development

Laboratory report) becomes involved in the early selection of new-product ideas because he meets with every design group during the third week of every month. The actual format depends on the design group; there may be either formal presentations by the design group leaders or informal discussion of problems.

Before an idea's feasibility is determined at semiconductor company A, the new-product business analysis (NPBA) form, which had been formalized six years before this investigation was done, is used. Marketing data are requested first on the form, including projected annual sales, nature of the device's existing competition, anticipated customers and usage, the marketing strategy the product follows, and whether and to what extent it makes present company A products obsolete (it should do so).

The NPBA form is filled out by someone working for the product group's marketing manager, and the information that appears on it is obtained either from in-house sales, engineering, and/or production people or from prospective users. The degree of confidence that the idea should be developed further is also required from the product group marketing manager and director, who must sign and date the form. The technical director then uses the form to screen new ideas. He does not know, however, how many new ideas are rejected before the prototype is made because he does not hear about them. This means that if the product group marketing manager and director sign the form, the idea is developed further.

The next step in reality-testing at company A is preparation of a prototype. Again, the NPBA form is used to record information about the new device as it is tested. The engineering portion of the form is filled out by product group engineers working on the project; it is signed by their section head, the design manager, and the director. Such estimates as design engineering, layout design, and test engineering times are required. In addition, a new-product electrical description sheet is completed and attached to the NPBA form. Only about 5 percent of new products are rejected for further development after the prototype is made.

Company C, like company A, puts primary emphasis on economic feasibility when it screens new ideas. Economic feasibility is tested first because technological feasibility-testing takes several months and management does not want to waste time and resources if no market for the product exists. The director of product planning becomes very involved in the economic screening. He deals with potential customers in determining their requirements and actually screens new-product ideas prior to feasibility-testing.

Two pieces of written justification are required during phase O, the pre-feasibility phase: the figure of merit (FOM) analysis and the design objective specification (DOS). The FOM is calculated by dividing costs into estimated revenue. Two important costs are estimated: "tooling" (engineering design costs) and "learning curve." If it costs $10 to make an item, but the company is only charging $5 to the customer in order to gain volume, the learning curve cost is

$5 until the firm learns to make it for $5. According to the director, a low FOM does not automatically disqualify the project for further development. There may be other strategic benefits promised, such as the fact that the product is but one step leading to another product with a higher FOM.

The DOS is a technical description of what the product is supposed to do. Although it is not very standardized, the same people tend to fill in the information for each project, and they do so along the same dimensions, so there is some consistency in the data obtained. The DOS data are gathered by talking to potential customers and thinking of applications. The DOS goes to designers in preliminary form and they comment on its feasibility, economic and otherwise. The written form and the discussion go back and forth until a final DOS is obtained.

One of the director's responsibilities is to insure that each step in the formal product-planning process is taken and that the FOM and DOS are prepared. He noted that prior to his joining the company two years before the study was done, no formal cycle existed at all. Instead, people filled out blank sheets on their progress. The development of the forms and convincing people to use them were still under way. It was taking a lot of work to get the forms accepted.

Prototypes are called "breadboards" or "mock-ups" in company C, as they are in the small appliance industry, among others. The director tries to force early consideration of the manufacturing process that will be used, as well as the kind of testing that will be done because the complexity requires it and the group could suffer later if they do not do such planning.

For instance, they might have to get new equipment and there is usually a delay in getting it. Also, the product might fit in with a number of others that will need similar equipment, so to avoid duplication and to get economies of scale, these data are collected as early as possible. This phase occurs about one year before actual production takes place. The director is aware that such early plans will inevitably change, however, and there is room on the form for indicating which revision is being considered.

Managing Feasibility Assessment

At this first decision-making phase of the innovation process, general management's role is to determine how formal and extensive the data-gathering procedures are, as well as to provide guidance about the organization's direction or strategy to innovators so that they can reality-test their ideas. The following observations, therefore, are limited to these features of reality-testing at the seven divisions as just described.

One of the striking differences between the semiconductor companies is that companies A and C require marketing and economic data about new ideas very early in the development process whereas company B, the most innovative in its subsample, does not. Similarly, pharmaceutical company F, one of the most innovative in its subsample, discontinued the practice of gathering preliminary quantitative commercial data about new products.

Company C (the least innovative of the three in the semiconductors subsample) had the most elaborate formal reality-testing procedure. Among the pharmaceutical firms, there was less variation in the ways in which this stage was structured. In all cases, quite formal systems were used. One reason for this is that the industry is so closely controlled by the Food and Drug Administration's safety and efficacy regulations.

In general, the reality-testing phase in each of these companies occurs in two parts: (1) prefeasibility or new idea screening and (2) prototype making and testing. Management (occasionally at least one or two levels above the scientists and engineers who come up with new ideas) participates in screening new ideas, and it is common for about half of these ideas to be rejected before a prototype is even made. It appears that managers themselves make the feasibility decisions instead of conveying the organization's strategy and allowing lower-level innovators to determine for themselves whether or not the new idea is feasible.

These examples should not be interpreted as illustrations of how to manage new-product development for radical innovation. As was noted in chapter 2, none of these companies had an innovation strategy that called for a large or frequent number of revolutionary new products. The examples do, however, provide fairly detailed descriptions of how formal reality-testing is done in industries where the costs of product development are substantial and the risks are great, partially because of such high development costs.

The Problem of Uncertainty

It has been noted that reality-testing is an attempt to reduce uncertainty about new ideas by getting more information about them and by comparing them to what already exists. The argument has been made that the less new the idea, as defined along the extent and timing dimensions, the less uncertainty there is about whether it will work. Therefore, there is less need for formal reality-testing of this kind of innovation.

At the other end of the spectrum of innovation, however, where new ideas are either radically different from what already exists or are considered for the first time, there is great need for formal reality-testing. The dilemma facing all innovators and managers who must decide about whether or not to support particular innovations is that just where the need is greatest, it is the most difficult to meet it. An integral part of the dilemma is the fact that there is little information about things that are radically different from anything that has existed before and/or that are coming into existence for the first time.

In the absence of information about a new idea, the condition of uncertainty, it is very difficult to predict whether or not it can be developed further, whether it will work as it is intended to, and whether, if it does work as it is intended to, it will be useful and accepted. Risk is the perceived probability of failure and its negative consequences; the greater the uncertainty, the more difficult it is to assign such a probability to a new idea. Assessment of uncertainty precedes assessment of risk. The two concepts are not the same, then, although they are related to each other.

For instance, there may be relatively little uncertainty about a new idea, such as introducing a new brand of shampoo to the existing market. There may be relatively great risk of failure, however, because the company introducing the new brand is small and without sufficient resources to widely advertise it, because of consumer loyalty to existing brands, and because most competitors are large and resource-rich. Conversely, there may be very little information (or great uncertainty) about a new energy source that enables engines to operate more inexpensively and for longer time periods on less fuel without harmful emissions, but very little likelihood that the new energy source will fail to be accepted in the marketplace. While examples such as these may be rare, they do indicate that, although it is common for uncertainty and risk to be highly correlated, the two conditions are distinct from each other.

Because it is so common for uncertainty and risk to be related to each other, it is natural to assume that uncertain things are risky, that they will not work, and/or that they are not feasible simply because not enough is known about them. Assigning risk at this early phase of innovation, however, is premature. It may be hypothesized, however, that is is just such premature assignment of high risk based on high uncertainty that historically has kept many revolutionary innovations hidden and unavailable to society for long periods of time. Instead of applying resources to radically new ideas to gather sufficient data about them to more rationally assign risk, it is easier for some people to dismiss uncertain new ideas out of hand.

It is possible, then, that the reality-testing phase of innovation will fail in its attempt to reduce uncertainty by providing more information about the new idea. The only information gathered from this effort may be that there is very little information available about the new idea and that there is very little comparable to it. In other words, its originator may not know for certain whether it is feasible or not. The new idea may be newer than its originator had realized.

However, this conclusion should not be interpreted as indicating infeasibility, meaning that the innovation process should end. Rather, it should mean that the idea's originator must become creative in either devising testing methods to try again to get information, or creating strategies for continuing development without sufficient evidence of feasibility. Both of these alternatives are methods for prolonging the reality-testing phase until a more definite conclusion about the idea's feasibility can be reached. Innovators who become committed to their ideas during their investigation of them have been known to persist in pursuing them for long periods of time despite lack of support, if not active discouragement.

It is often simply the passage of time that permits enough information about a radically new idea to accumulate to enable a determination of its feasibility to made made. The concept seems to be in limbo, waiting for its proper time to emerge. Thus, another outcome of uncertainty after reality-testing may be to put the idea safely aside, to be returned to periodically until enough data about it can accumulate to end this phase of innovation.

In the R&D division of a highly innovative photography firm, there is a great tolerance for what seem at first to be bad ideas, as long as their sponsors are honest about their progress and are aware of the risks involved. Researchers at all levels are given cut-off dates or time limits within which they can explore, but these limits vary. One sonar technique was explored for ten years before being introduced as the distinguishing feature of one very successful new product.

It is often difficult to enforce the cut-off dates at this firm, however, because few managers want to become unpopular. Sometimes, researchers are permitted to continue working on ideas until the last minute because managers hesitate to discourage them. Therefore, strong, trusting relationships are particularly important in order to avoid researchers' resistance to being told to stop working on an idea. And, even then, it is not unheard of for researchers to continue working secretly.

The point here is that during the reality-testing phase of innovation, the uncertainty surrounding a new idea is often first identified. Its discovery should not automatically mean that it is infeasible. Instead, the discovery of uncertainty means that the innovation process will probably take longer than may have been anticipated originally. The cost of a quick decision in the realm of innovation is often missed opportunities.

Some managers believe, however, that an important part of their job is to minimize, if not prevent entirely, the occurrence of failure in their organizations. It might be said, then, that managers are hired and paid to be risk-averse, if risk is defined as the likelihood of failure. In order for a high degree of risk to be accepted in most cases, there must be an equally high promise of reward. Thus, managers who are responsible for innovating or for managing the process of innovation are in an inherently difficult position. On the one hand, they are expected to be successful, but on the other, they are responsible for a process that is often marked by failure (much of which is unpredictable and unpreventable) and uncertainty about rewards.

Given this dilemma and the commonly recognized fact that innovation is most uncertain and fraught with failure at its earliest phases, it is generally best if management plays a restricted role at both the conceptual and reality-testing parts of the process. Unless top management strongly values innovation, there appears to be too strong a temptation for managers to bring to bear upon these stages the pressures that they feel for certainty and risk-reduction. One of the ways that some managers pass along their concern is to make unreasonable demands for numerical data, such as costs, completion times, and capabilities of the completed innovation. In some instances, it has been observed that such behavior may impede rather than stimulate the progression of a new idea's development.

Providing Information

Despite the belief that the managerial role should be fairly restricted and indirect during the early phases of innovation, there is one key function that managers can perform during the reality-testing phase. They can serve as passive sources of information.

Providing Information about Decision Makers' Needs. If there is a formal organizational procedure for evaluating and deciding upon requests for funds and other resources to further develop new ideas, then managers should be prepared to inform innovators about them, if they do not already know. If innovators do not seem to be aware of the procedures and do not ask about them, managers may lessen the shock that can come with reality-testing by casually mentioning the existence of such a formal system and by stating their availability to talk about it when the innovators are ready.

Management's attitude should be helpful rather than controlling at this point. The negative consequences of not adhering to the procedures or of not providing the information that decision makers will need to evaluate the ideas should be played down, while the purposes of the formal system and its benefits should be explicitly described. If preprinted forms are required for proposals, they should be used as the basis for discussion. A clear idea of management's requirements can help innovators streamline their information gathering about new ideas.

At the same time, however, managers should make it clear to innovators that if all the information required about an idea is not available or if it is only very approximate, it is still acceptable. If innovators perceive that only those ideas that can be concretely proven to be feasible will be considered by management, then they are unlikely to propose anything radically new, thereby depriving the organization of opportunities. A delicate balance, therefore, must be struck between getting enough information to warrant continued development and constricting the flow of new ideas with intimidating requirements for data that might not be available.

Management's providing innovators with information about its own information needs does not mean, however, that management should necessarily convey the specific criteria that will be used to determine whether new ideas are funded. If, for example, an organization typically supports new ideas that promise to generate a positive cash flow within a year, and management discloses this hurdle to innovators, there may be some tendency to come up only with ideas that can be demonstrated to clear it.

Such "playing to the standards" stifles creativity. Of course, if management is less interested in creativity than it is in keeping to its standards and it therefore really intends to support only such ideas, then disclosing the criteria communicates and reinforces its intention. An important part of exerting control is making goals and performance criteria very clear.

Providing Information about Strategy. Unless managers themselves are innovating (which they are more likely to do in the creation of new organizational forms and the adoption of new technologies), it can be said that managers generally have a better overview of how—if at all—new ideas fit into the organization's strategy than do the ideas' originators. Whether they take part in formulating strategy or not, managers should, and most do, have a fairly clear mental picture of what their organization's objectives and plans are, even if this picture is mostly inferential or intuitive.

Once again, management performs an important service to innovators by being open and honest about the direction in which it thinks the organization is moving, the organization's capabilities and limitations, and the extent to which new ideas conform to this "organizational reality." Additionally, if a particular manager suspects that his or her perceptions are not widely shared by other managers, then it is important to also disclose this information to inquiring innovators. It is vital if differing perceptions or beliefs are held by managers who may become involved in evaluating the new idea at some later point in its development.

Thus, management can play the role of political advisor to aspiring innovators, warning them of possible pitfalls, and pointing them in the direction of possible supporters. Representing organizational reality to innovators at an early stage can prevent them from becoming ensnarled in distracting conflicts that have less to do with the nature of the new idea itself than with the unit or person who has come up with it.[7] At the same time, however, managers should remember that the process is too young for them to "sign on" as supporters of new ideas. This is especially true if subsequently they will play a part in the evaluation and decision making about these ideas.

Providing Opinions about New Ideas. Maintaining the kind of neutrality toward new ideas at their reality-testing phase, as was just implicitly recommended, is difficult when innovators actively seek managers' opinions about them. Managers should remember, however, that at this stage, the task is to answer the question, "Can this idea be done? Is it possible?" but not "Is it good? Do you like it?" An innovator's simple question, "What do you think?" should be interpreted to mean, "Do you think this is a feasible idea?"

Many managers of innovation have achieved their positions precisely because of their technical knowledge and/or organizational experience. In most high technology companies, in fact, such managers have been or may continue to be innovators themselves. People with new ideas may view them as a source of expertise about new ideas and, thus, may seek them out as early sounding boards. If managers successfully play their role as neutral sounding boards at the early stages of innovation, they may not only gain a great deal of information about what their people are doing without having to ask for it, but they may also build the kind of trusting relationships with their employees that can pay off in other circumstances.

Again, in providing opinions about new ideas, managers must balance their responsibility to respond to innovators' inquiries with their responsibility to keep the process of information gathering operating as long as possible. Objectively and neutrally focusing on the facts about the new idea should prevent innovators from prematurely stopping the process by concluding that "My boss likes (hates) the idea. That's all I need to know."

The Outcomes of Reality-Testing

The outcomes of reality-testing appear to form a continuum ranging from clear feasibility to various degrees of uncertainty to clear infeasibility. What happens to any given new idea after its feasibility has been tested for the first time depends importantly upon these outcomes.

New ideas whose feasibility is certain are generally proposed as formal projects for funding. If the new idea is the adoption of a technology requiring the purchase or significant modification of facilities and/or equipment, then the innovation process may well intersect at this point with the capital budgeting system, if one exists formally in the organization. Generally, new ideas for products have their own funding mechanisms that are approached. No matter what the funding source or system is, however, if significant resources are needed to further develop a new idea, a formal written and/or oral proposal is commonly required in order to qualify for it. The next chapter examines the proposal phase.

As was noted earlier in this chapter, it is not always possible to get enough information about radically new ideas to determine their feasibility as soon as might be hoped. When uncertainty is the outcome of this phase, there appear to be at least four alternative courses of action: (1) return the idea to the conceptual phase for reformulation or revision and test for feasibility again, (2) push ahead with the idea in its uncertain state and try to get formal support for it based on grounds other than its immediate merit, (3) push ahead with the idea in its uncertain state without formal support, or (4) shelve the idea in its uncertain state, but protect it so that it can be reexamined periodically to determine if its feasibility can be more definitely determined.

Ideas that are clearly infeasible after their first screening are usually rejected, and their development process stops. Some companies keep files of such ideas so that future idea generators can consult them to stimulate their thinking.

While the reality-testing phase is not always an observable part of the innovation process, it can be a critically important phase under certain circumstances, regardless of the kind of innovation that is considered. It can represent the first time that management plays any formal role in the process, and it can set the tone for the way in which any given idea will evolve over time.

As is true with any kind of decision making, the more relevant, appropriate information that is gathered at this stage, the better the ultimate decision that will be made about the innovation. Such information may not be quantitative. Using numbers at the earliest stages of developing a very new idea, in fact, is often not only an exercise in futility, but it can be positively misleading.[8] Many managers looking for certainty tend to place too much faith in numbers, even if they sense that these numbers may have been pulled out of thin air by desperate employees. Such figures can result in a project that is like a house of cards—knocked over by its first brush with reality.

Therefore, when developing highly innovative new ideas, it is probably better to openly admit all the uncertainties and to live with them until the product, service, organizational form, or process concept itself gives rise to the key questions that must be answered before development or adoption can continue. In this way, the most meaningful, useful information will be collected as it is needed. A true picture of the concept's feasibility will emerge on its own.

Notes

1. Albert Rothenberg and Carl R. Hausman (eds.), *The Creativity Question* (Durham, N.C.: Duke University Press, 1976).

2. C. Merle Crawford, *New Products Management* (Homewood, Ill.: Richard D. Irwin, 1983), p. 328.

3. E. Patrick McGuire, *Evaluating New-Product Proposals* (New York: Conference Board, 1973).

4. Everett M. Rogers, *Diffusion of Innovations*, 3rd ed. (New York: Free Press, 1983).

5. Ibid.

6. For in-depth coverage of product concept testing, see Crawford, *New Products*, and Glenn Urban and John L. Hauser, *Design and Marketing of New Products* (Englewood Cliffs, N.J.: Prentice-Hall, 1980). For coverage of capital project evaluation, see Harold Bierman, Jr., and Seymour Smidt, *The Capital Budgeting Decision: Economic Analysis and Financing of Investment Projects*, 4th ed. (New York: Macmillan, 1975).

7. Rosabeth Moss Kanter, *The Change Masters: Innovation for Productivity in the American Corporation* (New York: Simon and Schuster, 1983).

8. The remainder of the chapter is reprinted with permission from my earlier work, *How to Manage the New Product Development Process*, p. 39. (Copyright 1982, American Management Association, New York. All rights reserved.)

5

Selling Innovation

A nyone who wants to do something new, no matter what it is, must at some point in his or her innovation efforts get the support of others in the organization. The selling phase of the innovation process represents the first concerted effort to introduce something new and to solicit various forms of acceptance and active support for its further development. The new thing is still in its early stages, an idea that has been tentatively determined to be feasible enough to pursue further.

In general, the selling phase occurs when development of the idea can only continue if more money, personnel, and facilities are allocated to it than are currently available. Proposals are the primary selling device. Although the smallest organizations are more likely to handle this phase informally, through oral conversations between innovators and management (if the two are distinct from each other), most organizations' management requires a written document.

The point in the innovation process when formal proposals are required varies, depending on the nature of the innovation and the size of the investment it requires. In some industries, such as pharmaceuticals, proposals are not written until after the first batch of the compound, or the prototype, has been made. In other industries, significant investment is needed before a prototype can be made; therefore, the proposal precedes that step. Some companies specify dollar expenditure ceilings, to go above which a formal proposal is needed. For example, one toiletries firm set a limit of $25,000 to be spent on development before approval was necessary to proceed further.

The purpose of this chapter is to present an integrated view of the proposal phase of innovation that includes not only the perspective of the originators of innovation, but also that of its evaluators and potential adopters. It is assumed that as the originators approach the task of getting funding and other kinds of support, it is useful for them to be aware of potential adopters' point of view. Similarly, as adopters approach the task of allocating resources for innovation, it is helpful for them to recognize the originator's perspective. Because proposals are a form of communication between proposer and evaluator, mutual awareness of the other party's point of view increases the likelihood of accurate sending and receiving of information.

The Importance of Selling

To some idea generators, formulating a proposal may appear to be merely a procedural necessity, an irritating requirement for detail to be dispatched as rapidly as possible so that the more important developmental task at hand can continue. This kind of attitude may prevent many good ideas from receiving the attention and support that they deserve.

Such an attitude can result in so much resistance to the task of preparing the proposal that whatever creativity is needed to make it the best one possible is blocked. The proposal phase is important enough to elicit the same kind of creativity that was used to come up with the innovation itself. When this phase's value goes unrecognized, however, poor proposals are common. Therefore, the proposal phase frequently represents the end of the development process.

Proposing to do something new often takes a great deal of courage. The very nature of innovation is to improve upon or to deviate from what exists. Thus, proposing an innovation implies dissatisfaction or disagreement with the status quo. Such negative attitudes pose a threat to anyone with vested interests in what exists. If this implicit conflict is played out in the form of an innovation that is ultimately accepted and implemented, then innovation is indeed a destructive process.[1] It destroys the status quo. Proposers of innovation, therefore, must expect at least some opposition, if not ridicule and dismissal. Not only may an innovation itself be inherently risky, but the very act of proposing it also may be risky for its originators' self-esteem, if not their careers.

When innovating is viewed as purposeful conflict with the status quo, in whatever form it takes, the proposal itself can become analogous to both sword and shield. The proposal announces the intention to do something new, and it implicitly attacks what exists. At the same time, it can be used to protect the new thing by making claims for its superiority, even its indispensability, over what exists. The greater the conflict the proposal stirs, and the less protection it provides, the more likely it is that the innovation will not be adopted, regardless of its merits.

The proposal phase of the innovation process is also critical because it serves so many purposes. From the viewpoint of the new idea's originator, who may not be conscious of having any negative attitudes toward the status quo, the proposal is the vehicle for the innovation's first formal debut in the larger organization. On the other hand, from the perspective of the decision makers representing the interests of the larger organization, the proposal presents yet another potential use of resources, regardless of the degree to which it threatens the existing order. Still, some evaluators may view a proposed innovation as an opportunity for greatness, rather than as one of many competing drains on scarce time, money, and personnel.

Additionally, the activity of preparing a proposal can serve as a way of bringing together a variety of groups from a range of organizational functions. The collaboration necessary for this task, if well guided, can help to integrate the disparate parts of the organization by giving the people working on the proposal a first-hand knowledge of the goals, time frames, values, and ways of handling conflict that characterize other organizational units.[2]

If the completed proposal is routed to a variety of departments' managers, as was done routinely for new-product proposals in several of the consumer firms in the research project upon which this book is based, then it serves as a notice of what projects are in the works. The recipients of proposals may be asked to attach written comments or questions about the estimates and possible problems before passing the documents along.

The opportunities for consultation provided by this mechanism will frequently result in further improvements in the character of investments actually submitted to the final decision makers. In any case, it will provide valuable information for top management in weighting the important intangible factors almost invariably associated with an investment proposal.[3] Such a practice, however, can be time-consuming. Furthermore, if it is used without interdepartmental collaboration in actually preparing the proposal beforehand, it may arouse managers' anxieties as they discover the possible implications for their own departments' work load or access to resources.

The problems and potential conflicts, therefore, may surface after the proposal is complete, thereby reducing its chances for acceptance or causing it to be sent back for more work to those who prepared it. It appears, then, that using completed innovation proposals as information devices across departments may only work under the following conditions: (1) the innovation proposed is not terribly new, (2) it has relatively few, minor, or positive implications for a variety of departments, and (3) there is no rush to continue the project's development.

The proposal phase of innovation serves the function of bridging the levels of the organizational hierarchy. The formal procedure of submitting innovation project proposals can educate innovators about the major strategic factors affecting their particular concerns. Nonetheless, it is not enough for upper-level managers to wait for innovation plans to bubble up from lower levels. If general management does not intervene, the sum of initiating-level plans can become a "meaningless catalogue." Thus it is an important way for general managers to influence the innovation process.[4]

Joseph Bower found that capital projects are defined at the lowest levels of the organization during the "initiating phase." Projects are then submitted to middle-level general managers, such as division general managers in large firms, during the "integrating phase." At this point, management decides whether to support the project and to provide impetus for it to be pushed further up the hierarchy for ultimate approval. He found that at the corporate executive level, the project is basically rubber-stamped.[5]

Finally, a formal proposal for innovation, if accepted, can serve as a kind of agreement between the new thing's originators and its adopters. That is, the proposal becomes a formal record or charter of what has become the project.[6] As a charter, the proposal contains objectives, plans for achieving them, estimates for performance, and an early sense of the degree of uncertainty associated with this innovation. The proposal, then, functions as a reference and source of guidance, especially for long-term projects in which there may be personnel turnover.

Principles of Proposing Innovation

Considering the latent conflict commonly associated with suggesting anything new, and assuming, therefore, that not everyone who learns about the new thing is going to want it, proposing innovation can be likened to selling something to customers who are not at all sure they want it. Proposals, then, are sales pitches. Writing them can be a highly specialized task. Indeed, large high technology firms, such as those in the aerospace and electronics industries, whose survival depends upon successfully selling their ideas to get government contracts, typically have full-time proposal-writing staffs as part of their marketing department.[7]

If proposal writing is another form of selling,[8] then many of the essentials for effective salesmanship should be applicable to this phase of the innovation process. Among the most relevant of these requirements are: (1) knowledge of the proposal's evaluators and their needs, (2) explicit description of the innovation's importance and how it meets decision makers' needs, and (3) proof that the innovation can and will meet decision makers' needs.

The following guidelines can be used by general managers to convince their superiors or boards of directors to approve innovations. They can also be used to sell new ideas downward to lower-level groups that did not initiate the new idea, but that must cooperate in implementing it.

Principle 1: Knowing the Audience

Market research as a field of endeavor is based upon the assumption that consumers choose those things that best satisfy their needs, and that if something is to sell, it should satisfy the needs of at least some consumers. Discovering what these needs are takes varying degrees of investigation (which the field of market research is trying to make scientific), depending upon how similar the seller is to the buyer and upon how regularly the seller has direct contact with the buyer. By observing buyer behavior first-hand, the seller is more able to make accurate inferences about what buyers really want. The more similar sellers (proposers) are to buyers (decision makers) and the more frequent their contact, the less necessary is formal data gathering about buyers' needs. Under such conditions, the proposer should already know, perhaps intuitively, what will motivate the decision maker to accept the proposal.

Those organizational members who make decisions about innovation have a variety of needs, some of which may be inferred from the nature of their position in the organization as well as from their task of decision making. Not all of these needs, however, are rational and conscious. Some are emotional and unconscious, as when a decision maker has a great need for the esteem of peers, but is unaware of it and would probably deny it if confronted with the observation.

Among the needs of decision makers that result from their position in the organization are: (1) to carry out organizational objectives and (2) to meet or exceed organizational standards, while remaining within certain limits. For example, a division general manager or functional vice president may feel the need to reduce waste and cut operating costs when the larger organization's objective is to consolidate and strengthen its current market position. At the same time, however, this decision maker also wants to maintain the reputation for rapid, courteous service that has developed over time. Training expenses and bonuses for staff, however, must be kept within tight limits.

As representatives of the larger organization and stewards of its welfare, decision makers should be motivated by proposals demonstrating the ways in which their innovations will permit decision makers to more successfully fulfill their roles. Continuing with the example of middle managers in the consolidating organization, a proposal is more likely to capture their attention if it begins by promising that the innovation will somehow enable the quality of service to remain high at lower costs without increasing staff training or incentives. It is just as important for those proposing new ideas to be aware of their organizational context at the proposal phase of innovation, then, as it is at the earlier phases of this process.

The task of making decisions about innovations is another source of inferences about what a proposal evaluator's needs might be. In general, decision makers must choose from among a variety of competing proposals. The most rational way of making this choice is to compare the proposals across a number of criteria that are weighted according to their importance. Proposals that contain the information necessary to make such comparisons motivate evaluators to give them serious consideration. In fact, if the proposer knows the criteria that are likely to be used to judge innovations' acceptability, then the general presentation can be tailored to clearly show how the particular innovation excels in meeting the most important criteria. For example, the proposal could begin by claiming to meet these criteria, and the most important data supporting these claims could be highlighted and given a prominent position in the document.

Another way of thinking about discovering the needs of those who will be evaluating a proposal is to learn what their main problems are. In the governmental contracting business, contractors generally receive a "request for proposal" (RFP) from potential buyers. This document describes the buyer's needs or the problem to be solved by the potential contractor. Inadequate analysis and understanding of this problem, as displayed in the proposal, is a common reason for rejection.[9] While it may be unusual for the originators of an innovation in other kinds of organizations to receive a tangible statement of a problem, using this "strategic" approach to organizing the proposal may increase its chances of at least capturing the evaluators' attention.

Principle II: Establishing the Innovation's Importance and Benefits

By knowing the audience's needs, proposers of innovation can gain its initial interest at a more emotional level.[10] Simply diagnosing the audience's needs, however, is not enough to increase the likelihood that the proposal will be accepted. This analysis must be translated into action by taking what is assumed, known, and predicted about the innovation and expressing it in terms of the innovation's importance and benefits.

Essentially, an innovation should be important to, or valued by, decision makers because it helps their organization to meet its objectives. Although it may not be necessary, or even appropriate, to state these objectives in the proposal itself, they should provide the organizing principle for stating the reasons why the innovation is important.

For example, in organizing this chapter, it was assumed that not all readers think that the proposal phase of the innovation process is important enough to warrant an entire chapter. In order to capture all readers' attention, therefore, a section at the beginning of the chapter argued that proposals themselves are important in innovating because poor ones can delay or stop the process regardless of the merits of the innovation itself. Underlying this argument were the ideas that many readers need to be able to prepare effective proposals, and that many readers need to be able to understand what goes into making a proposal so that they can make better decisions about them.

Generally speaking, it is in describing the innovation's nature and function that its importance and benefits become apparent. In addition to using the organization's objectives and other strategic features (such as problems to be solved) as guidelines for what should be included in this section, referring to the innovation typology in chapter 1 may also be helpful. As displayed in table 1–1, an innovation's importance can be derived from its function, its extent of newness, and/or its timing. The benefits come from the specific ways in which the innovation improves quality, for example, or is a simple variation of what already exists.

Returning to this chapter's design as an illustration of how a proposal could begin, its benefits were described in the introduction. It claimed to be useful to a wide variety of readers because of the different points of view it would assume, as well as because of the different kinds of innovation to which it could be applied. The introduction also argued for the utility of the chapter to follow by promising to provide some principles of effective proposing and some examples of how other companies handle the proposal phase of innovation. In many ways, the introduction of each chapter of this book is a miniature proposal, attempting to gain the reader's attention and acceptance of the ideas that it contains.

Principle III: Proving the Innovation's Claims

Although logic alone rarely sells anything, without it to support the emotional appeals that capture potential buyers' interest, it is less likely that sales will be made. Most buyers need to think of themselves as being rational; thus, they want proof that they can believe the claims that have been made. Proposals, then, should persuade their evaluators that the innovation will be and do what it promises and that, therefore, investing resources in it is a good decision. Logical arguments are generally characterized by a statement of purpose, an explicit discussion of key assumptions upon which the argument is based, a series of assertions (each of which is supported with factual evidence), and a conclusion.

If the purpose of a logical argument is to prove an innovation's credibility, then there are a number of ways to be credible. One way is to provide as much detailed, quantitative data about the innovation as possible, including such graphics as tables, diagrams, blueprints, and plans.[11] Another approach to establishing credibility is to demonstrate the experience of the idea's originators in carrying out similar innovations or show the tasks involved in implementing the innovation.

In most instances, relatively inexperienced innovators must be able to produce a demonstrably superior idea in order to gain organizational support. Having a mentor or sponsor with credibility who can either assist in proposal preparation or act as a preliminary, informal evaluator can become an important success factor at this phase of innovation.

Because the more radically new an innovation is, the more important credibility is, it may be well to hold off on the proposal phase of such innovation until feasibility in at least some form can be established. It is paradoxical that the newer an innovation is, the more information about it is needed to convince potential adopters, yet the more difficult and expensive it often is to get such information. This is one reason why radical innovations can be a decade in the making. Not many resources may be available for the data gathering needed to create a winning proposal for a substantial infusion of money and personnel.

There have been reports of individuals who believe in the new idea without hard data using their own personal resources, dipping into unit "slush funds," or working "under the table" with unauthorized organizational resources in order to keep the innovation process alive until a formal proposal can be written.[12] In some companies, managers know that such clandestine projects or "skunkworks" exist, but turn their heads, hoping that they will produce an innovation in spite of, rather than because of, the organization. In fact, in semiconductor company C, the director of planning expressed a wish for more such under-the-table work.

Proposals as Managerial Control Devices

There are a variety of ways in which innovation proposals can be used to insure achievement of the organization's performance objectives, which is the primary purpose of managerial control systems. By notifying management that something new (a product, process, service, or organizational form) is in the offing, proposals provide information about activity at the lower levels of the organization, where most of the new ideas are generated. The people who have generated the ideas and are proposing their development also come to management's attention.

Such information makes management aware of the degree to which its innovation goals, if any, are being achieved. For example, some high technology companies expect that almost 100 percent of their sales in, say, five years, will be derived from currently developing new ideas. The information that an innovation proposal provides also alerts management to the way in which resources are being used and how much it is costing. With such data, managers can better determine how well the organization's limits are being respected.

In addition to supplying data about current organizational activities, innovation proposals enable managers to plan for future achievements and expenditures. Future needs for capital and other resources can be projected from the proposals. Furthermore, accepted proposals can be used as guidelines for costs, deadlines, and other forms of structure surrounding the innovation. For capital projects, proposals can be used in comparing actual experience and costs. Some experts believe that the discipline of making such comparisons keeps proposers honest in estimating vital figures.[13]

Assuming that the more information about innovation management has, the more control it can exert over it, there are several ways to use proposals specifically to increase control. The first method is to specify the kinds and amount of information that the proposal must contain. The second method is to require proposals to be submitted early in the innovation process, that is, before very much money has been spent on a particular idea. A third way is to require that written proposals be accompanied by an oral presentation so that evaluators can question sponsors and proposal writers (if these are not the same people) about the contents of the written document. Yet another approach is to require that proposals be resubmitted during the course of development to reflect major changes.

The Form of Innovation Proposals

Meeting the needs of those who read proposals should be the primary objective in designing their form. By form is meant the way in which a proposal's contents are organized and presented. Proposals' forms can vary greatly in terms of the order in which the data appear, the data's volume and detail, the degree of formality characterizing their preparation and presentation, and the writing style used. This presentation will focus on ways of thinking about form itself rather than on any one form as being better than another. It will consider who determines proposals' form and the degree of formality because these are the most relevant aspects for general managers.

Designers. Three different approaches can be taken to determine what form proposals should take. One approach is for those who review proposals to design them. Another approach is for those who prepare them to determine what they will look like. The third approach is for proposers and reviewers to negotiate a format ahead of time. Each of these ways of proceeding has its pros and cons.

When those who read proposals dictate their form, there is greater likelihood that because they know their own needs best, they will design a document that provides them with enough of the right kind of information for good decision making. There is also a greater chance of standardization of forms, thereby making it easier to compare proposals. Such standardization and predetermined categories of information, however, may encourage proposers to gather enough of only the prescribed kind of data to satisfy the form. Alternatively, proposers may feel the need to distort what information they consider to be important, but that is not called for, in order to fit what is required.

On the other hand, if the proposers are permitted to design their own forms for organizing and presenting data about their own innovations, they can highlight the new idea's strengths and make the best possible argument. This may decrease the likelihood that a truly promising innovation will be rejected simply because its economic attributes are either too uncertain or not quite up to standard. Standardization can scarcely be expected, however. Therefore, comparison of proposals may be made very difficult for evaluators. Furthermore, evaluators may get much more information and detail than they want or need, especially if competing proposers begin to try to outdo each other in their presentations.

The third alternative is for proposers and evaluators to collaboratively design the form that will be used in proposing innovation. Evaluators can specify what their information needs are for decision making, and they can present these to proposers as guidelines. Proposers can suggest modifications, such as more opportunity for qualitative description. When those who have generated or first become aware of the new idea are also the proposers, they are able to exert more control over what happens to their idea if they can be instrumental in determining the proposal's form.

Ability to retain some control can be particularly motivating for some individuals, especially those who feel that the new idea is "my baby," and who are consequently reluctant to let go of it or to entertain suggestions for changing it. Such participative management may help to prevent the kind of game playing that can detract from this phase of innovation when too much managerial control is exerted over it, but it is more time-consuming. Both parties may view the negotiations process as just so much administrative detail that neither wants to pursue.

Degree of Formality. Another issue to consider in deciding upon the form that an innovation proposal should take is how formal it should be. Formality may be measured in a variety of ways, including whether or not the proposal is written; how glossily it is written; whether or not standardized, preprinted forms are used; whether or not it must be resubmitted if major changes occur in any of the major assumptions; whether or not written proposals must be accompanied by an oral presentation; and whether or not a different group of people than the innovations' originators prepare proposals.

Formality is frequently equated with bureaucracy, and is generally considered by students of organizations to be an attempt to make organizational processes of any kind (including innovation) more rational, objective, and controllable rather than emotional, subjective, and uncontrollable. Formality, then, especially in the innovation process, is an effort to reduce proposals' political nature.

Because most organizations are hierarchical in their authority structures (meaning that top management makes the most important decisions and determines what the lower levels of the organization should do), top levels of management typically decide how formal the innovation process will be. In fact, top and middle management's role in this phase of the innovation process is generally restricted to determining whether proposals are required at all and how formal they will be. These levels of management rarely become directly involved in proposal preparation itself.

The pros and cons of a high degree of formality in the innovation process in general have been debated by researchers and academics. One point of view is that formality is necessary and good; the other is that it stifles innovation and, therefore, is bad. Formality has been advocated because it is believed to prevent the development or adoption of half-baked ideas that turn out to be either failed new products or services or else white elephants stored in the adopter's "attic."

By minimizing politics and maximizing logic, it is believed that innovation can be made less wasteful and more certain than it is if allowed to progress naturally.

Opponents of formality, however, claim that not only is it time-consuming because of all the routines, procedures, and documentation that it requires, but that it is also expensive and that it will not necessarily reduce uncertainty and waste or increase efficiency in innovating. Furthermore, it is believed that the prospect of such requirements discourages potential innovators from following through with their ideas. Formality is also thought to distract innovators from their primary task of creating or introducing new things and, by doing so, to frustrate them, thereby reducing their motivation, satisfaction, and, ultimately, their creativity.

Some researchers have hypothesized, in fact, that high degrees of formality are not appropriate for the task of innovation because of its ever-changing, unpredictable nature and because of the nature of the self-motivated, authority-challenging people who usually are the innovators in organizations.[14] The lack of fit between the task, the people, and the degree of formality is believed to result in less successful innovation.

Unfortunately, there is no conclusive evidence to prove the accuracy of either point of view. One of the findings of the research upon which this book is based is that at least in developing new products, all of the companies studied (including the most successful in developing new products) tended to have some formalities in their innovation process. No company, however, strictly enforced procedures and written documentation at every phase. Although they varied in which aspects of innovation they conducted informally, even the firms that were least successful as innovators did not try to control everything about new-product development.

The innovation proposal is generally the first opportunity that management has in many organizations to truly influence the degree of formality used in developing or adopting innovations. Individual managers' needs for detail, comprehensiveness, and polished appearance will partially determine the degree of formality this phase of the innovation will have. The precedents set by the larger organization, however, are by far the most important determinants. In some cases, external forces (such as government agencies requiring certain kinds of tests for new products) also establish requirements that must be met, thereby shaping the form a proposal will take.

In general, the larger the organization, the more levels of management, the more competing demands on the organization's resources, and the scarcer these resources, the more likely it is that the proposal phase of the innovation process will be characterized by a high degree of formality, as required by top and middle levels of management. On the other hand, the smaller the organization, the fewer its levels of management, the fewer competing demands for its resources, and the more abundant these resources, the less formal this, or any, phase of the innovation process is likely to be.[15]

Examples of How Proposals Are Used

A variety of approaches have been taken to the proposal phase of the innovation process. Among the non–high-technology consumer firms participating in the pilot study upon which this book is based, one company did not use written proposals at all, while another used an elaborate procedure for writing them. In the next section, a sample of these firms' procedures will be described, followed by a description of the procedures used by a sample of the high technology companies discussed in previous chapters.

The Non–High-Technology Companies

The least formally managed company in this sample was the importer and manufacturer of silver plate and pewter hollowware and giftware, cutlery, and crystal. The firm's new-product strategy was to make lower-priced copies of competitors' new products and to use pricing as its chief competitive weapon. There was very little risk involved, since all items introduced already existed in the general market, and only those that were selling well were selected to be copied.

Assuming that control systems by their very nature are designed to reduce uncertainty, it might be expected that this company's management of innovation was fairly informal. Without a specialized new-product department, it relied primarily upon salespeople to bring in items that they had seen in retail outlets, advertisements, or trade shows. An informal committee met on Saturdays and some evenings to discuss them. The president and founder, the executive vice president, the manufacturing vice president, and representatives from the sales and purchasing departments were usually present at these discussions. An already-existing item was analyzed to determine if it could be made less expensively with different materials. No preprinted forms were used, nor was a proposal of any kind necessary.

Some of the company's manufacturing managers could estimate within 2 or 3 percent the cost of making almost anything. These estimates and the item's identification number were written down, and a salesperson took the description to a retailer and asked if it could be sold at a certain price. Then the retailer's normal margin was factored into the formula, and the company was able to determine what its profit margin was likely to be. If six months or more were needed for lead time, the cost estimate was increased by 5 percent, as a rule of thumb. The pressure then was placed upon the purchasing department to maintain the estimated cost structure and to get the product or component at the proper time. These procedures were not written down and were purposely kept flexible in order to respond to customers' needs.

A new product usually could be developed and delivered in three months. The ten-year–old company had higher sales and sales growth (an average of 20 percent per year) than had its higher-priced, more established competitors; its earnings had increased by 36 percent in the year preceding this study. The average earnings growth rate for even the most successful, more traditional firms was approximately 6 percent.

At one of the largest companies in the beverage industry, which had introduced three new products in the past five years compared to one apiece for its major competitors, the new-product manager could spend up to $10,000 on exploring an idea and assessing its business opportunities. Before any significant market research funds could be spent, however, the firm required a pro forma proposal concretely identifying its economic potential.

The manager spent about 20 percent of his time collecting information about new-product ideas, with help from the market research and manufacturing departments. He estimated most figures used in the pro forma proposal, except cost figures. These estimates were refined when more information became available as development proceeded. Thus business analysis, concept development, manufacturing and quality assurance, and preliminary consumer analysis could all be done for approximately $10,000. The first management evaluation, requiring a more formal proposal, was done before the advertising agency was brought in to develop copy, graphics, and a brand name. Thus, estimates and proposals were required at a moderately early phase of development.

The most formally managed new-product development occurred in a large company in the cosmetics and toiletries industry. Each business within the company's personal care division had its own new-product development staff, for a total of eight new-product managers. These managers had to obtain approval of their objectives for their new ideas before any funds could be spent on testing, according to the divisional controller.

After a new idea had been conceived and tested with consumers, new-product managers sent a "personal care division research and development project request" form to the R&D department. The form required that the manager assign a number to the project and state the reasons why an opportunity existed and the expected growth size, in addition to desired product attributes, desired claims, packaging, target direct cost, and desired timing of the project. The vice president of marketing also signed this sheet.

When R&D either affirmatively or negatively responded to the request, it indicated the amount of money and labor needed, whether or not it had budgeted for the project, and the project's impact on R&D's facilities and other projects. Once R&D approved the project, records were kept of all expenses and R&D time devoted to it. These were reported on a monthly and year-to-date basis for each project. Presumably, the market research department had already kept records of expenses incurred for consumer concept testing before any project was submitted to R&D for its acceptance.

Before $25,000 was spent, a "corporate new-product proposal" had to be written by the new-product's manager, who was expected to gather information for it from the R&D, sales, manufacturing, and operational planning departments. The proposal required financial assumptions and analysis, trial/volume analysis, projected market research and R&D costs, a summary of results of work done to date (such as consumer scans or focus groups), and marketing strategies. The proposal was sent to the division's vice presidents of R&D and marketing, the controller, and president for their approval.

Although some proposals were next submitted to the corporate group level's approval cycle, as long as the division's president had signed off on it, the project was completely funded for divisional activity. Consumer concept testing and between six and eight months of laboratory time could be purchased for $25,000. Given the average development time of two years, the proposal had to be filled out at the end of the first quarter of first third of the development process. The formality was heightened by the need for a written R&D request, which was in itself a type of proposal preceding the one used for managerial evaluation.

The High Technology Companies

Table 5–1 contains a summary of the extent to which seven companies used proposals to control new-product development. Both semiconductor and pharmaceuticals firms required written proposals in order to justify making proto-types of new products. In the semiconductor industry, however, it was more common to require formal justification even earlier in the innovation process. One reason for this is that making new integrated circuits often requires new manufacturing equipment, whose acquisition must be planned as far in advance as possible.

The pharmaceuticals companies were more likely to require oral presenta-tions and more than one formal proposal to continue development of new prod-ucts than were the semiconductor companies. Some of this difference is due to the fact that development of drugs takes three to four times as long as does the development of integrated circuits. There is more opportunity for change that management needs to know about. Also, there is simply more time to spend in preparing oral presentations because the development pace is slower, and the product will have patent protection after it has been introduced, thereby re-ducing the need to move quickly to keep ahead of the competition.

Although it was very unusual for the controller's or financial vice president's approval to be needed on proposals in any of these companies, it was common for their managers to compare actual new-product performance to estimated per-formance as forecast in proposals. This practice is recommended by Harold Bier-man and Seymour Smidt as a way of preventing overly optimistic projections from being made by advocates of new ideas. It also helps to establish individuals' track records in accurate estimation, which either enhances or detracts from their credibility in future proposals.

Despite the similarity of practices among the seven companies, there were some notable exceptions. In semiconductor company B, for example, the amount

Table 5–1
Proposals as Control Devices in Seven High Technology Companies

Description of How Proposals Are Used	Semiconductor Companies			Pharmaceuticals Companies			
	Co. A	Co. B	Co. C	Co. D	Co. E	Co. F	Co. G
1. Written proposals are required in order to build a prototype.	5	3	4	4	5	5	4
2. Written proposals are required before prototypes are built.	5	3	4	1	1	1	4
3. More than one proposal must be submitted for any new product.	1	2	2	2	5	3	5
4. An oral presentation of new products is required to get approval.	3	2	2	5	5	5	3
5. The controller or financial vice president must approve all proposals.	1	1	1	1	1	3	1
6. Actual new-product performance is compared to estimated performance as forecast in proposals.	5	4	4	4	5	5	4

Notes: 1 = never (loosest control); 2 = rarely; 3 = sometimes; 4 = most of the time; 5 = always (tightest control).

of written justification needed depended upon the hierarchical level of the source of the new-product idea. If the general manager wanted a new concept developed, no written proposal was necessary. If the idea came up from a low level, however, a great deal more written material was needed.

In semiconductor company A, which required written proposals very early in the development process, a new-product business analysis form (NPBA) had to be completed even before the idea's technical feasibility was assessed. Therefore, assessment of commercial and economic feasibility preceded technical feasibility assessment, and the NPBA served as a proposal to determine technical feasibility. Every new idea had to be written up. The technical director used the forms to screen new ideas. He did not know, however, how many new ideas were rejected before the prototype was built because he did not hear about them. If the product group marketing manager and director signed the form initially, the idea was developed further.

In pharmaceutical company F, the divisional controller had to occasionally approve proposals, an unusual example of tight managerial control. Part of the reason for this was that, according to the divisional director of business planning, corporate-level management was "paranoid" about the pharmaceuticals division because it was a high-risk, high-return business that generated relatively few new products. The corporation also had low-risk, low-return businesses in its portfolio, and it did not know how to handle the differences in risk levels among them.

In addition to determining the degree of managerial control exerted over innovation by using proposals, this analysis also measured individual R&D scientists' and engineers' perceptions of the proposal-writing requirement. These perceptions were then compared to the respondents' levels of innovative behavior in order to learn the nature of the relationship, if any, between perceptions of this type of managerial control and creativity.

Table 3–4, questionnaire items 6 and 10 display the company averages of individual respondents' perceptions about two aspects of proposal writing: the importance of written justification for pursuing new ideas and the use of accurate estimates as a basis for evaluating their job performance respectively. In general, more of the pharmaceuticals scientists perceived that written justification was important than did the semiconductor engineers, with the exception of respondents from pharmaceuticals company D.

On the other hand, more of the semiconductor engineers perceived that they were evaluated on the basis of their accuracy in estimating the performance of their new products than did the pharmaceuticals scientists. Despite the fact that this performance criterion is commonly used by companies in both industries, it appears that only the semiconductor companies' innovators tended to be especially aware of it.

As table 3–5 reveals, no very strong relationships were found between either of these measures of perceived managerial control and innovative behavior. Nonetheless, new-product developers whose ideas had been used tended to perceive that they were evaluated on the basis of how accurate their new-product estimates turned out to be once their product was introduced to the market. Once again, the fact that idea use was higher in the semiconductor industry, in which respondents were more likely to perceive that they were evaluated on this basis, may mean that industry affiliation explains part of this relationship. It has the highest coefficient in the matrix, however ($r = .35$), which indicates that at least the opposite relationship is not operating in the drug industry.

Respondents' perceptions that they are judged on the accuracy of their estimates about how well an innovation will actually perform may indicate that in their divisions, their track record of success with past ideas is an important determinant of whether or not their present ideas are actually used. Furthermore, it indicates a sense of accountability among respondents. If they think that it is important for them to be accurate, they may only come up with ideas that are easy to make estimates about, that is, ideas that are not radically new. This explanation fits the semiconductor industry, where incremental innovation is the norm. On the other hand, people in both industries may only put forth an idea after they have enough information about it to accurately estimate how well it will do, thereby making it seem more worthy of being used.

Based on the results of this analysis, it may be tentatively concluded that the perceived importance of written justification for further developing new ideas has little to do with individuals' innovative behavior. Awareness of the importance of being accurate in estimating how these new ideas will perform in the marketplace, however, may well encourage innovators to propose only those ideas about which they know they can accurately make predictions. If a company's innovation strategy, then, calls for an emphasis on evolutionary new services, products, or other kinds of innovation, it appears that one way to encourage evolutionary innovation is to make clear the importance in proposal preparation of accurate estimates of performance, costs, and deadlines.

It appears that in developing new products, at least, all of the companies studied, even the most innovative, tended to have some formalities in their innovation process. No company, however, strictly enforced procedures and written documentation for every phase of it. Although they varied in which aspects of innovation they conducted informally, even the firms that were least successful as innovators did not try to control everything about new-product development.

As a control device, the proposal used to communicate new ideas to management for its use in making decisions is considered necessary by many organizations. Rather than stifling innovation, such formality can actually enhance the likelihood that an idea will be given a fair evaluation. If done well, proposals can assist in the kind of good decision making that avoids both kinds of failure associated with innovation: implementing useless new ideas and ignoring useful ones.

Notes

1. Robert H. Hayes and William J. Abernathy, "Managing Our Way to Economic Decline," *Harvard Business Review*, Vol. 58 (July-August 1980), pp. 67–77.

2. Paul R. Lawrence and Jay W. Lorsch, *Organization and Environment* (Homewood, Ill.: Richard D. Irwin, 1969).

3. Harold Bierman, Jr., and Seymour Smidt, *The Capital Budgeting Decision: Economic Analysis and Financing of Investment Projects*, 4th ed. (New York: Macmillan, 1975).

4. Joseph L. Bower, *Managing the Resource Allocation Process* (Homewood, Ill.: Richard D. Irwin, 1972).

5. Ibid.

6. C. Merle Crawford, *New Products Management* (Homewood, Ill.: Richard D. Irwin, 1983).

7. Herman Holtz, *Government Contracts: Proposalmanship and Winning Strategies* (New York: Plenum, 1979), p. *v*.

8. Dorothy Leonard-Barton and William A. Kraus prefer the term *marketing* in their article "Implementing New Technology," *Harvard Business Review*, Vol. 63, No. 6 (November-December 1985), p. 103.

9. Holtz, *Government Contracts*, p. 99.

10. Ibid, p. 126.

11. Ibid.

12. Thomas J. Peters and Robert H. Waterman, Jr., *In Search of Excellence* (New York: Harper & Row, 1982).

13. Bierman and Smidt, *Capital Budgeting Decision*, p. 276.

14. Lawrence and Lorsch, *Organization and Environment*; Jay W. Lorsch and John J. Morse, *Organizations and Their Members: A Contingency Approach* (New York: Harper & Row, 1974); and Bengt Sandkull, *Innovative Behavior of Organizations: The Case of New Products* (Lund, Sweden: Studentlitterature, 1970).

15. Tom Burns and G.M. Stalker, *The Management of Innovation*, 2nd ed. (London: Tavistock, 1966).

6
Selecting Innovation

During the selection phase of the innovation process, proposals to innovate are evaluated and either accepted or rejected. Although new ideas have been the subject of a variety of decisions prior to this stage of their development, it is at this point that the most critical decision is made about innovations' fate. Will they get whatever they need to continue development and implementation? For the first time in the process, organizational managers commit themselves to innovate by accepting proposals for funding because they agree to invest significant sums of money and other scarce resources.

This is also a critical point in innovation because, although the idea's originators can exert influence on the organizational decision makers, they do not have the authority to actually make the decision. In other words, the idea's originators give up control at least temporarily, and in some instances, for good. The organization's management ultimately determines what happens to an innovation.

While the previous chapters have focussed on the activities of new ideas' developers as a way of enhancing managers' understanding of how innovation occurs, this chapter shifts to the activities of managers themselves. It is at this point in the innovation process, then, that management moves to the center of the stage and actually makes the decision. It is assumed, however, that management reacts rather than takes the initiative. Management has been summoned to play its part by the proponents of the innovation, although (as indicated in chapter 5) the point in a given innovation's development when proposals are submitted varies.

This is not to imply that managers themselves cannot generate and develop new ideas to solve organizational problems. They can and do. In such cases, managers call upon their superiors to react to their proposals during the selection phase of innovation. The term *management*, then, is generic in this chapter and refers to those decision makers who have authority to allocate the resources needed to complete the innovation, regardless of who originates it.

In other words, evaluators' location in the authority hierarchy varies, depending upon who originates the innovation and the organization's size and degree of decentralization. The closer to the top the originator is and/or the smaller and more centralized the organization is, the more likely it is that top executives will evaluate and select innovations. On the other hand, the closer to the bottom of the organization the originator is and/or the larger and more decentralized the organization is, the more likely it is that decisions will be made at middle levels, by division or group general managers.

Some Assumptions

Several important assumptions underpin this chapter's analysis, each of which will be discussed briefly. The first is that there are commonalities in the way that decisions are made about all types of innovation because selecting innovation can be thought of as a special case of decision making in general.

As a class, however, innovation decisions are unique in two important ways: they best exemplify the difficulties of deciding under conditions of uncertainty, and their impact is destructive of the status quo. Finally, at this point in the innovation process, decisions take the form of selection from among competing alternatives for allocating resources. Therefore, they are primarily economic decisions.

Whether the particular innovation being decided upon is a new product, a new way of processing materials, or a new sales training program, decision makers perform many of the same kinds of cognitive steps. All types of innovation decisions require managers to assimilate information about the innovation, to apply at least one criterion to what is known about the innovation, and to determine the extent to which the innovation meets it. If it does meet the stipulations, it is selected for further development and implementation. This is the most basic process, which is not necessarily rational.

The most rational way in which to make a managerial decision, particularly an economic one, is to gather as much information about the innovation as possible. This includes identifying alternatives to it (including that of doing nothing) and what the positive and negative consequences of each are likely to be. To judge the innovation, more than one criterion should be used. The criteria should be derived from the objectives of the broader organization. Because some of these criteria may be in conflict with each other, each should be weighted to reflect its relative importance to the organization.

The criteria should all be applied to each alternative, each alternative should be scored to reflect how well it measures up to the criteria, and the alternative with the highest score should be selected. To insure objectivity in assessing the extent to which an alternative meets the criteria, several decision makers should evaluate and score it. Then, the average of these scores should be taken and compared to average scores of other alternatives.

Research on human decision making reveals that very few decisions are actually made this way.[1] Instead, information gathering and alternative generation tend to cease as soon as an alternative that meets enough of the criteria has been found in a process termed "satisficing."[2] Furthermore, the criteria applied come from a variety of sources, not just organizational goals. Decision makers may not be aware of these goals or may not agree with them. Criteria may be more closely related to their own personal needs, some of which may be unconscious. Sometimes only one criterion is used.

Selective perception, in which the decision makers see or hear that which they need or want to see or hear plays a large part in the extent to which an innovation is judged to meet criteria.[3] Weighting and scoring, if done at all, are done implicitly by individuals.

Despite the underlying similarity that unifies all kinds of decision making, selecting an innovation is a unique experience. By definition, something new is to some extent unlike that which exists. Therefore, the information about it that a decision maker has available is often quite limited. Decision makers may not know whether or not the new thing meets all of the criteria of acceptability or if it ever will. In the absence of objectively verifiable information, other factors (such as decision makers' values, needs, and perceptions) become dominant. Therefore, deciding about innovation can be much less rational than other kinds of decision making, and no amount of mathematical modelling will make it any more so. What one does with limited information does not change the fact that it is limited.

Another feature of innovation decisions that sets them apart from many other kinds of decisions is their disruptive potential. Doing something new, whatever it is, often means losing something that currently exists. This loss can be viewed as very destructive to organizational members, including the very managers who are required to make the decision. In fact, the more personally disruptive the innovation is perceived to be, the more threatening it is, and the more defensive decision makers may become. Not surprisingly, threatened decision makers do what they can to destroy—or at least to undermine and delay—new ideas.

Even if the decision maker is not in the least bit threatened by the innovation, and in fact, very much wants it to happen, the fact that it may disrupt other organizational members' status quo means that a decision to go ahead with something new can be quite unpopular. Thus, in deciding about innovation, managers often face more issues around the decision's acceptability to others than they do with other kinds of decisions. Gaining compliance with their directives may be more difficult.

Requests to fund innovation projects often do not come to managers in an orderly progression, segregated from other requests for resources. Top managers may be presented simultaneously with several different kinds of innovation opportunities, ranging from replacing existing computing facilities with the latest model of personal computers to starting a day-care center for employees' children. At lower levels, division general managers or marketing department managers may need to choose which new-product projects to fund, and manufacturing vice presidents may have to select which kind of new processing equipment to purchase and install. It is unusual that innovation decisions are made all at once during the same time period.

The innovation decision, then, is generally but one of many decisions that any given manager is called upon to make during any given time period. Sometimes, there are other comparable innovation opportunities to select among, but sometimes, there are not. In this case, the decision may be more one of deciding whether to innovate or to do something else with the resources. A complex web of other decisions often provides the context within which any one innovation selection is made. The nature and outcomes of these other decisions can have a direct bearing upon the way in which the innovation request under consideration is handled.

Thus, managers who are in a position to select innovation often find themselves immersed in making other decisions at the same time, some of which may be related to their predisposition toward the innovation. Such situational complexity does not make selection any easier. Furthermore, in addition to the difficulties of making a quality decision due to inadequate information, managers of innovation face the difficulties of gaining organizational acceptance due to potential disruption.

It is no wonder, then, that there are so many poor innovation decisions. They may be the toughest choices that managers make. Yet, if made badly, new things are tried that should never have been attempted and they fail. Huge sums of money are wasted. An even more serious error, however, may be that too few attempts are made to do new things that need to be done. Organizations lose their ability to adapt to their changing environments and begin to decline. Entire industries may be affected, as are economies and societies.

Making decisions about innovation, therefore, can have very wide- ranging, long-term implications. Managers have a great responsibility to make them well. Over the past decades, more and more techniques have been developed for making more rational innovation decisions, based upon the assumption that rationality is best. Yet, when innovations cannot meet the requirements imposed by rationality, they are abandoned, sometimes permanently, with the harmful effects noted above.

Furthermore, study after study reveals that many managers do not use these sophisticated techniques, despite the fact that many of them have been available for years.[4] It is almost as if practitioners resist becoming more rational. What could the reasons for such recalcitrance be? Surely it is not lack of intelligence, training, and experience!

Using the principle of "requisite variety" from the field of communications theory (which holds that in order for a message to be received accurately and clearly, the receiver must have as much variety as the message has complexity),[5] managers should consciously use all of their cognitive facilities (including both logical and intuitive ones) in evaluating and selecting something as complex as innovation. Using logic without intuition leaves managers seriously imbalanced in their approach to innovation decisions.

Political Processes in Selecting Innovation

The traditional economic view of resource allocation holds that decisions are made by an individual at the top of the organizational hierarchy. In reality, however, it is more often true that many important decisions are made long before top management receives a request for funding. Lower-level managers, then, in effect screen possible alternatives, thereby determining those from which higher levels of management may choose.[6]

Furthermore, rather than relying solely upon economic criteria, it is more realistic to think that general managers decide upon which innovations to sponsor by evaluating the track record of the proposer as well as the quality of the project. They must believe the sales forecasts justifying the income projected. They must accept its technical claims. Individual general managers also estimate the benefits to themselves of being "right" and the costs of being "wrong" in selecting projects.

These estimates are based on the decision maker's answers to such questions as: What is my job history and likely future? What are my skills seen to be? What will be my next job? How soon will it come? What is the innovation's history? What kind of issues were involved in its earlier development? Who was involved? What are the rewards for cooperation? What are the penalties for unsuccessful projects in my area?[7]

Much of the political process described above has been corroborated by a more recent study of a number of various-sized firms. Among the political factors considered in screening capital investment proposals were: the extent to which the manager or division originating the project needs "either encouragement or compensation for some previous defeat," the desire not to embarrass the chairperson or president of the firm by sending a carelessly reviewed project to the board of directors, the credibility of the project's sponsor, the ability of the sponsor's division to generate profitable projects, the strength of the case the sponsor makes for the project, past experience with the sponsor and the sponsor's division based on "postaudits of projects made and reported," and the ability of the sponsor to make good estimates.[8] This latter criterion was also found to be important in the fieldwork on which this book is based, as described in the previous chapter. That is, it appeared that new-product developers whose ideas were used tended to perceive that they were judged by the accuracy of their estimates.

Shifting to a more specific treatment of the politics of innovation, Rosabeth Moss Kanter's model of the process includes the "coalition building" phase, in which the idea originator's ("entrepreneur's") immediate boss and higher-level managers decide whether or not to support the project being "sold." Although Kanter adopts the perspective of these entrepreneurs, her observations about the ways in which superiors are persuaded are instructive about how decisions are made.

Kanter found that it is important that each decision maker be made to feel as if he or she were "THE most important one for the project's success." One-on-one meetings between the entrepreneur and the decision maker seemed to be effective not only because they fostered this feeling, but also because they permitted the decision maker to influence the project's design.[9] From this observation, we can infer that such personalized selling can help the idea's originator to become aware of, if not to overcome, the decision maker's feelings of being threatened.

Individual meetings can also prevent the mistake of bringing together people who are doubtful about the idea so that they can learn that they are not the only ones with worries about it. Furthermore, successful entrepreneurs adhered to the "rule of no surprises," meaning that they avoided introducing at meetings information, requests, or problems for which they had not already prepared the attendees. The implication here is that group dynamics importantly affect decision making.

In the last step of the coalition-building phase, top management endorses the innovation, thereby inducing others to join together as supporters. In her study, Kanter found that to give this endorsement, high-level decision makers appeared to want very specific requests made in formal proposals. In some instances, decision makers were concerned about their own ability to sell the project to their superiors, typically the board of directors, another key factor in whether or not they decided favorably upon the project.[10]

According to most traditional views of the best way in which to make innovation decisions, interpersonal influence, whom one knows, and one's credibility and affiliations all seem to be the wrong reasons for accepting or rejecting an innovation. Rejections based on these political grounds may seem terribly unfair. Yet, relying upon these factors, at least in part, may be quite sensible.

Political processes provide a kind of information that may corroborate or contradict proposals, which, it can be assumed, put the innovation in its best possible light. Thus, politics can be functional for reducing an innovation's inherent uncertainty. It acts as a check on the sales, costs, and development time estimates in a way that is difficult to manipulate.

Political processes also are functional for gaining acceptance of new ideas by directly addressing decision makers' feelings of being threatened by the innovation. Interpersonal contact and credibility enable innovations' proposers to better demonstrate their good will and deference toward decision makers as well as their ability to make good on their promises about the innovation. Gaining the support of at least a few influential people also helps the innovation to gain acceptance by those who must implement it. The force of sheer numbers increases peer pressure which can overcome resistance to changing the status quo.

While it is important for rational techniques to be used to select innovations, paying attention to the political reception they receive is also important. Something that looks good or bad on paper can take on a very different appearance when subjected to political forces. Something that looks bad on paper because it is radically new and cannot meet rational criteria may turn into something very good if enough organizational commitment for it can be gained. Only political processes can make this happen, and they may well explain how breakthroughs ever occur.

Group Processes

In many organizations, innovations are selected by groups of decision makers: boards of directors or trustees, offices of the president or director, and executive committees, for example. While it may only be the largest and most important innovations that are decided upon by such groups, the very fact that it is these key innovations that are so handled indicates that some attention should be paid to how group dynamics can influence decision making.

Despite Bower, Kanter, and others' conclusions that most important decisions are already made before they bubble to the top of the organization, few groups of managers are this level will openly admit that they are only rubber-stamping them. Their members prefer to believe that they are performing a vital task. Otherwise, why waste their time? Therefore, most groups will at least discuss proposals submitted to them before formally reaching consensus or voting.

During this discussion, the way in which the group operates as a group, apart from the decision-making task, can play a critical role in: (1) whether a decision is actually made at that meeting, (2) the nature of the decision (such as approval or rejection of a proposal), and (3) the quality of the decision in terms of whether it is in the organization's best interest.

When individuals, especially those who have achieved high levels of power in organizations, come together to make decisions, they tend to bring with them their own, often unconscious, agendas that may have very little to do with the new thing under formal consideration at the meeting. These private, or "hidden," agendas can include such items as: appearing well informed, if not expert; gaining favor with or competing with the group's leader; gaining other members' acceptance of the individual's ideas; maintaining harmonious relationships between the individual and select others, or among the entire group; and minimizing the amount of time spent in the meeting. Additionally, members generally have relationships with other group members outside of the decision-making group. These relationships are brought into the decision-making arena and can be the basis for coalitions or conflicts that can distract members from the task at hand.

Several theories of group dynamics describe and explain the "invisible" processes that can occur in decision-making groups. The most psychological theory, devised by Wilfred Bion and developed by the members of the Tavistock Institute, holds that groups' dynamics depend, in part, upon the attitude toward authority that each member brings into the group. It can be positive, negative, or ambivalent. The agglomeration of these attitudes plays an important role in the way in which the group behaves toward its formal leader (if it has one), toward the emergence of an informal leader if it does not, and toward each other.

These combined attitudes towards authority result in the group acting as if its members are: (1) very dependent upon or independent of the leader, (2) escaping from something, quite often the task or the leader, because they are threatened in some way by either of these "culprits" or fighting with something, again, either the task, the leader, or each other, or (3) coming together to produce a magic panacea for the future.

Each of these conditions is termed a "basic assumption." When groups are behaving on the basis of any of them, they are less likely to be concentrating upon selecting an innovation, even if on the surface it appears that the topic of discussion is the innovation. What happens is that the task at hand—instead of being the end or purpose of the meeting—becomes the means toward the end of the group acting out its basic assumption, whether it is dependence, fight-flight, or pairing.[11]

While this theory explains why groups often do not make decisions when they are supposed to or make poor ones when they do, other theories of group development indicate that the best decisions will only be made after the group has spent enough time together to reach the "individual differentiation" or "collaboration" stages. These are the fourth and last stages of development. In the individual differentiation stage, decision making is based on individual expertise, goals are understood and accepted, and the group is confident and satisfied. In the collaboration stage, relationships are supportive and open, people speak freely and are committed to goals, listening and information sharing are good, disagreement is resolved as it occurs, while decision making is collective when all resources are needed, but individual when there is one expert.[12]

Before these stages are reached (which can happen rapidly if the group spends frequent concentrated periods of time together, but which may never happen at all), other issues are of more concern, as indicated by the following titles of the stages. The first is "membership," in which participation is superficial and polite and decision making is dominated by more active members. The second is "subgrouping," in which decision making is fragmented and deadlocks are common because members have found safety in clusters that differentiate themselves within the group. The third is "confrontation," in which decision making is based on power, with frequent disagreement and hostility among subgroups.

On the other hand, if a group becomes too well established, the very cohesiveness necessary to permit it to focus on the task of deliberating about an innovation can also prevent it from making a high-quality decision. The "groupthink" phenomenon occurs when individual members censor their own opposing criticisms of the dominant opinion in the group in order to preserve the good feelings of cohesiveness.[13]

Groupthink is related to the "risky shift" phenomenon observed in some groups.[14] This heightened willingness of the group to accept greater risks than individual members would accept if they were to decide individually generally occurs under the following conditions:

1. Responsibility is believed to be spread around the group so that no one member can take blame for failure;

2. The members feel more confident about alternatives because of the greater amount of information available from each member;

3. The more dominant, vocal members of the group are also the greatest risk-takers;

4. Group members are not in competition with each other; and

5. The group is relatively large, but cohesive.[15]

Given the risk inherent in most innovation decisions, it can be inferred that groups making such decisions would be most prone to the risky shift phenomenon. Despite its drawbacks, group decision making can be very effective when it functions properly. Doing so means that every member of the group not only brings, but also willingly uses, a wider range of information and problem-solving skills for the task of deciding upon an innovation than any one individual decision maker could. The underlying principle of group decision making is that "several heads are better than one," because of every individual's limitations and special abilities.

This principle is particularly true in selecting innovations because the far-reaching implications they generally have for all departments and levels of the organization are critically important factors in determining whether or not they are good for the organization as a whole. These ramifications can best, and sometimes only, be identified by members of those affected units, however.

Nevertheless, it has been found that pushing back individuals' limitations and inducing effective group work depends importantly upon two factors: (1) the quality of leadership and (2) the group's willingness and ability to manage its own process.

The best leaders of decision-making groups tend to be those who not only pay most attention to the invisible group dynamics, but who also restrict their use of authority to controlling these dynamics so that they do not derail the group's efforts to make a decision. Such leaders have been observed to exert this control in a variety of ways, including: insuring that everyone participates as equally as possible, defusing tension and hostility, reminding members of goals and norms, and preventing members from withholding or withdrawing from the discussion.

Other important functions that effective leaders perform are: informing members in advance of the topic(s) to be discussed and insuring that the agenda is adhered to in the decision-making session; heightening information exchange and mutual understanding among members; testing members' comprehension and checking on the group's progress toward reaching a decision; and assessing whether or not the group is close to achieving consensus.[16]

Group decision-making leaders who impose their opinions on their group generally cause the kinds of dysfunctional dynamics previously described. Quite often, group members resent having their time wasted in making a decision that the leader clearly has already made. They may feel manipulated by being asked to play a game. Yet, if the leader takes too passive a role, these dynamics can also erupt. Thus, leaders of decision-making groups must find the proper balance of control and freedom for their groups if the group itself is not to become a negative factor in decision making.

Most groups are either unaware of their own processes or reluctant to take responsibility for them because they do not know what to do about whatever problems occur. Professional process consultants and trainers have been used in some organizations to educate groups so that they can take responsibility for themselves.[17]

Group processes, like political processes, can be functional for choosing innovations because they increase information and, therefore, certainty not only about the innovation itself, but also about its ramifications for the organization. Group processes also permit more people to become involved in making the decision, which overcomes resistance to doing something new by giving the participants more of a sense of owning it. Furthermore, the risky shift phenomenon enables organizational members to undertake more risk than they would as individuals. If rational techniques are used by well-operating groups, then, the combination can go a long way toward improving innovation decisions.

Individual Psychological Processes

A High-Involvement Model

The individual manager who must decide whether or not to fund an innovation is in many ways in the same position as consumers who must decide whether or not to spend their money on a new product. Consumers and managers have a variety of ways in which their limited resources can be allocated; they are uncertain about whether the innovation will deliver on its promises; and they will pay a penalty for making a poor decision.

Research on consumer behavior has applied general decision and motivational theories to develop a process model of consumer decision making that is relevant for this analysis of how innovation decisions are made. Figure 6–1 presents a composite diagram of psychological factors that influence consumer decision-making behavior.[18] The model is an adaptation that has been tailored specifically for decision making about innovation in organizations. It will serve as the basis for the following analysis, which extends beyond consumer behavior and draws upon other disciplines as well.

When people are highly motivated to achieve a goal by making their decision, and they consider their decision to be important, they are termed "highly involved." As a result, their thinking is believed to be different than it would be if they were more passive and felt less responsible.[19] Whatever their hierarchical level, managers who are most responsible for selecting innovations for their organizations are assumed here to engage in high-involvement decision making. In other words, the analysis that follows applies to those managers whose decisions generally carry the most weight and are rarely, if ever, reversed by their supporters.

Starting at the bottom line of the diagram, the likelihood that an innovation is chosen from among alternatives (intention/decision), is believed to be determined by the person's attitudes toward that particular innovation. These atti-

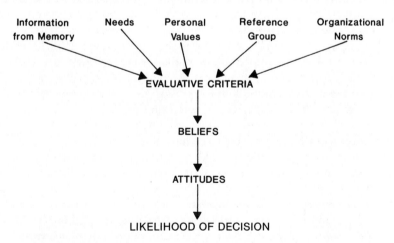

Source: Adapted from James F. Engel and Roger D. Blackwell, *Consumer Behavior*, 4th ed. (New York: Dryden, 1982), pp. 416, 442.

Figure 6–1. High-Involvement Decision Making

tudes are learned predispositions to respond consistently in a favorable or unfavorable manner with respect to that alternative. In turn, these attitudes result from the decision maker's beliefs, which consist of information that connects the selected innovation to important evaluative criteria. In other words, the decision maker thinks that the innovation does or does not have certain desired attributes.[20]

It should be noted that what is being explained here is simply the likelihood that the decision maker will select a particular innovation. James Engel and Roger Blackwell are careful to point out that despite statistically sophisticated research techniques, no decisive evidence has been found to indicate that attitudinal changes cause directly corresponding changes in behavior.

Among the reasons for the model's inability to predict actual behavior are that it does not explicitly include: (1) the myriad anticipated and unanticipated circumstances that affect choice (such as availability of goods and money to pay for them), and (2) pressure to conform. These factors have been touched upon in this chapter's previous sections on political and group processes as factors in making decisions about innovations.

As figure 6–1 indicates, the key to deciding about innovations is the set of evaluative criteria that are used. The bases for the criteria appear in the top lines of the diagram. They include information from memory plus needs, personal values, reference group influences, and organizational norms.

Developing Evaluative Criteria for Selecting Innovation

Evaluative criteria are standards of acceptability that reflect what the decision maker wants to get or achieve by investing in the new thing. In general, people have many reasons for the decisions they make. Consumer behavior studies reveal that consumers generally use six or fewer criteria to evaluate alternatives, although under some circumstances as many as nine may be used. The more involved the decision maker, the greater the number of evaluative criteria that tend to be used. Also, more-involved decision makers are more reluctant to consider alternatives that differ very much from these criteria.[21]

Information from Memory. Managers may remember what happened to similar types of innovations in the past, and from these memories they may develop some things that they either want to avoid or repeat as they evaluate the present innovation. For example, a manager might remember that when a similar type of decision to adopt new office equipment was made several years previously, it was based on overly optimistic estimates of how long installation would take. Delays resulted in prolonged, unanticipated disruption to her department.

Based on this memory, she may use as a criterion for judging this most recent innovation her trust in the proposer's estimates about such things as length of time needed to implement it. Answers to the questions raised in Bower's political model (such as "what is the innovation's history, what kind of issues were involved in its earlier development, and who was involved?") also come from memory and can generate criteria. Conversely, if the manager remembers that it was widely acknowledged that one of the reasons why this new technology eventually worked so well was that the manufacturer's service representatives were very responsive and efficient, then she is likely to use as another criterion the availability of manufacturer's support in judging the merits of the currently proposed innovation.

Thus managers' experience in evaluating and selecting innovations is an important source of criteria. It can be a very costly source, however, because managers learn from mistakes as well as from successes.

Individual Needs. According to most motivational theories, one of the factors that makes individuals unique is their differing predominant needs. While most theorists agree that all human beings have both lower-level needs related to our species' survival and higher-level needs related to our more highly developed brains and self-awareness, there is little agreement about what specific needs should be called, their priority or relative urgency, or whether, in fact, identifying and organizing them is even possible or useful.[22]

Nonetheless, their clinical experience and empirical research have enabled some psychologists to develop hypotheses that shed light on the kinds of needs that appear to be predominant among managers. David C. McClelland's work on the higher-level needs for achievement and power in managers is particularly relevant for understanding how they develop criteria for choosing innovations. The most effective managers are those whose strongest need is for socialized power, defined as the need to influence other people, win in competition, and attain a position of greater authority, primarily for the benefit of others and for the manager's organization.[23] These individuals find their greatest satisfaction, then, in getting other people to achieve societal or organizational goals.

Managers in whom this need is strongest would be likely to develop criteria for evaluating innovations that have to do with the extent to which the innovation puts the organization at a significant advantage over its competitors, or the extent to which the proposer adheres to organizational strategy and procedures in putting his or her idea forward.

For example, a manager with a strong need for socialized power might decide upon a proposal to enter a new market with strained foods for elderly people by assessing how well the proposal conformed to company guidelines for estimating sales and return on investment. He might also use the criterion of how much of an increase in market share entering the new segment would provide. This power-motivated manager might also judge the proposal on the basis of how well informed its proposer had kept him during its earlier development.

McClelland and Burnham found that the most effective managers also had a strong need for achievement, although it was not as strong as their need for socialized power. McClelland defines the need for achievement as that which is satisfied by doing things better, making improvements, attaining challenging goals, completing difficult tasks, and meeting standards of excellence.[24] These goals, tasks, and standards do not need to be related to the person's organization. People whose need to achieve is stronger than any other need generally consider the goals to be so important that they may not trust anyone else to work toward them, preferring to take complete responsibility for them. This inability to delegate causes problems in organizations and is why the best managers' need structures subordinate the need for achievement to the need for power.

Other research on leadership and managerial motivation corroborates McClelland's work. John B. Miner found, for example, that the factors most closely correlated with managerial success were (1) a positive attitude toward superiors' use of authority, (2) a need to compete, and (3) a willingness to tell other people what to do, as well as to back it up with rewards and punishment.[25]

Ralph Stogdill's profile of the most successful managers and administrators, culled from two reviews of all the leadership studies done since 1904, reveals needs for responsibility and task accomplishment. Goal-orientation, creativity in problem solving, taking charge in social situations, self-assuredness, stress resistance, and tolerance for frustration are other characteristics.[26]

Many of these traits overlap with those of innovators, suggesting that managers can be innovators themselves, as well as judges of innovations. Criteria that might evolve from these traits and needs would be those focussing on the nature of the innovation itself. Is it, in fact, an improvement? Is it of highest quality? Will it actually solve a problem or bring something to completion or resolution?

People with the high need for achievement revealed in these profiles also tend to pay attention to the amount of risk posed by an innovation. Although most managers do not distinguish between the concepts of risk and uncertainty, theorists define risk as the estimated probability of success or failure and uncertainty as inability to estimate a probability.[27] McClelland has found that people with strong achievement needs prefer to take on projects that have about a 50–50 chance of being accomplished successfully because they pose enough likelihood of failure to be considered as a challenge, but not so much challenge that failure is too likely. Fear of failure is the negative side of need for achievement.[28]

Nathan Kogan and Michael Wallach's research on the personality traits and needs associated with risk taking shows that regardless of the decision maker's gender, the need for independence or autonomy was strongly linked to willingness to take risk. In terms of correctly assessing the riskiness of a decision, people with little fear of failure and a relatively weak need to maintain a positive image to other people (nondefensiveness) were best able to discriminate among different kinds of decisions and to gauge the degree of risk taking accordingly.[29] In general, however, people are inconsistent and highly biased in subjectively estimating probabilities.[30]

For example, familiar, recent, or emotionally compelling events are usually most easy to imagine as occurring. Therefore, we tend to overestimate the likelihood that they will occur in the future.[31] It could be inferred, then, that a decision maker who had recently or painfully experienced the failure of a past innovation attempt would tend to overestimate the risk posed by a current innovation proposal.

Other research has found that younger managers tend to be more willing to take risk than their older counterparts.[32] The strong negative relationship between managers' age (which ranged from 22 to 58 years in the analysis) and risk taking held regardless of whether managers were in marketing, finance, personnel, R&D, engineering, or general management.

Related to this finding is the discovery that inexperienced people tend to take greater risks than their more experienced counterparts.[33] Additionally, most people are willing to take bigger risks when the stakes are perceived to be low.[34] In other words, if failure does not appear to be costly, people are more inclined to take risk. Furthermore, higher risks will be accepted if it is believed that one's organization is relatively invulnerable to irregular environmental changes.[35]

The amount of risk, or probability of failure, posed by an innovation, then, is generally considered to be a central criterion in evaluating whether or not resources will be allocated to it. How managers calculate these probabilities and how low they must be in order to be considered acceptable are highly individual matters. Despite the amount of research conducted on how people make decisions, no "laws of choice" have been established.[36]

Personal Values. An individual's values are his or her ideals of right and wrong, good and bad, importance and unimportance. Managers' values can be critical determinants of the criteria applied to selecting innovations. In their study of managerial risk taking, Victor Vroom and Bernard Pahl note that managers tend to assess themselves as being more willing to take risk than their peers because they value risk taking.[37] Another more recent survey found that younger managers place more importance on money, ambition, and risk than do their older counterparts.[38] Thus, an innovation's riskiness would emerge as a criterion from the values source as well.

Studies of values commonly held by the most effective managers indicate that pragmatism is primary. Also, traits such as ambition, achievement, and creativity are considered to be prerequisites for success.[39] Pragmatism as a value leads to such evaluative criteria as the innovation's usefulness, its ability to solve real problems, its contribution to efficiencies such as cost savings and economies of scale, and its potential to increase productivity. The value of innovation for its own sake would predispose managers favorably toward anything new, but the prevailing pragmatism of management in the United States limits this positive attitude. In fact, the very definition of innovation includes usefulness. Just because something is new does not mean it is an innovation. It must be usable to qualify.

Reference Group Influences. Managers' reference groups within their organizations are the units of coworkers with whom they most closely associate themselves. If the manager is currently in a finance department or has spent much of a career performing financial functions, for instance, this person may view other finance managers as the reference or "home base group." Note that this home base group generally differs markedly from any group that forms to ultimately select innovations. Most such decision-making groups are interdepartmental or cross-functional. In this section, the focus is on these basic departments and functions.

A manager's group affiliation can be the source of criteria for evaluating innovations because each department within an organization has its own goals, short- or long-term time horizons, task- or relationship-oriented interpersonal relationships, and degree or formality in its structures and procedures. These differences generally emerge from each department's required function within the organization and the degree of environmental uncertainty it faces.

This uncertainty is measured by the clarity of information the environment provides to the department, how straightforward causal relationships are in knowledge needed to operate within the department, and the length of time before the environment provides definitive feedback on how well the department has performed. The less clear and straightforward the information the department has to work with, and the longer it takes to get feedback, the greater the uncertainty. Lawrence and Lorsch found that because they face the greatest environmental uncertainty, the most effective R&D departments, for example, were characterized by relatively less formal structures and procedures, and longer time horizons than the production or marketing departments in their organizations.[40]

To continue with the example of the finance manager, his or her group may have the goal of insuring that the organization's monetary assets are used as efficiently as possible. Gaining the greatest return for the least investment is considered to be important. Conservative, cautious behavior that befits responsible stewardship of the organization's money is likely to be expected of all members of the group.

It is not difficult to imagine what kinds of criteria a manager from this group would use to evaluate an innovation. The costs and cash flow needed to implement it, its impact on other capital projects, and its dollar savings or profitability are criteria likely to be applied.

Organizational Norms. Norms are internalized standards of acceptable behavior that all members of the group or organization believe that they should observe. The function of norms is to maintain and enhance the unit. The more well established and cohesive the unit, the more likely it is to have a set of norms that are well enforced.[41] Examples of organizational norms are: to at least act as if saving money is a good thing, to wear sportclothes to work, to come in to work on weekends, to socialize with coworkers after working hours, and to listen respectfully to new ideas, no matter how far-fetched.

Organizations' objectives and methods for achieving them (their strategy) can be an important determinant of the norms that emerge. If, for example, a company's strategy is to grow rapidly by developing and introducing as many new products as it can over the near term, then such norms as asking members at all levels of the organization for new ideas, listening patiently to all new ideas, and displaying willingness to try anything once may emerge and apply to everyone in the company. Criteria for judging new-product proposals that are formally submitted in such a company, then, might take the form of the innovation's potential to gain rapid consumer acceptance or its ability to complement or build upon other innovations.

Organizational norms frequently emerge from the values and life-style of its leadership. As this individual or group demonstrates and talks about their values and their preferred ways of doing things, they are disseminated throughout the organization. Organizations that have been founded by inventors or entrepreneurs who place great value on innovation and risk taking typically have them as norms. Organizations in which it is acceptable behavior to take risks—and to avoid punishing those who do take risks but who fail in their innovation attempts—generally are most innovative.[42]

Norms can be consciously established or changed by leaders who consistently model and reinforce the desired behavior. To be considered a norm rather than a rule, however, the attitude and behavior must be introduced and enforced informally over a relatively prolonged time period. Once established, norms become part of members' way of viewing their organizational existence. Norms slip out of their awareness and only become noticable again when someone violates them. Because they become habitual, however, norms can be difficult to change. Thus, revitalizing an older, bureaucratic organization having norms of little risk taking and innovation can be a formidable, but nonetheless possible, task.

Individual decision makers may have more vision or higher performance standards than their organizations. Making unpopular decisions that deviate from organizational norms may be necessary in troubled organizations. Much depends upon the integrity and intentions of the individual. A decision that appears to be irrational from the point of view of a majority of organizational members may, in fact, be in the best long-term interests of the organization.

Notes

1. Bernard M. Bass, *Organizational Decision Making* (Homewood, Ill.: Richard D. Irwin, 1983), pp. 4–8.

2. R.M. Cyert and J.G. March, *A Behavioral Theory of the Firm* (Englewood Cliffs, N.J.: Prentice-Hall, 1963).

3. D.D. Dearborn and H.A. Simon, "Selective Perception: A Note on the Departmental Identification of Executives," *Sociometry* (June 1958).

4. Bass, *Organizational Decision Making*; C. Merle Crawford, *New Products Management* (Homewood, Ill.: Richard D. Irwin, 1983); and Lawrence J. Gitman and John R. Forrester, Jr., "A Survey of Capital Budgeting Techniques Used by Major U.S. Firms," *Financial Management* (Fall 1977), pp. 66–71.

5. W. Ross Ashby, *An Introduction to Cybernetics* (London: University Paperbacks, 1964).

6. Joseph L. Bower, *Managing the Resource Allocation Process: A Study of Corporate Planning and Investment* (Homewood, Ill.: Richard D. Irwin, 1972), pp. 15–16.

7. Ibid., pp. 56–58.

8. R.M. Cyert, M.H. DeGroot, and C.A. Holt, "Capital Allocation within a Firm," Technical Report No. 109, (Pittsburgh: Carnegie-Mellon University, May 1976).

9. Rosabeth Moss Kanter, *The Change Masters: Innovation for Productivity in the American Corporation* (New York: Simon and Schuster, 1983), p. 217.

10. Ibid., p. 223.

11. Margaret J. Rioch, "The Work of Wilfred Bion on Groups," in Arthur D. Colman and W. Harold Bexton (eds.), *Group Relations Reader* (Sausalito, Calif.: G.R.E.X., 1975), pp. 27ff.

12. Allan Cohen, Stephen Fink, Herman Gadon, and Robin Willits, *Effective Behavior in Organizations*, 3rd ed. (Homewood, Ill.: Richard D. Irwin, 1984), pp. 145–147.

13. I.L. Janis and L. Mann, *Decision Making* (New York: Free Press, 1977).

14. Nathan Kogan and Michael Wallach, *Risk Taking: A Study in Cognition and Personality* (New York: Holt, Rinehart and Winston, 1964).

15. Bass, *Organizational Decision Making*, p. 140.

16. Gary A. Yukl, *Leadership in Organizations* (Englewood Cliffs, N.J.: Prentice-Hall, 1981), pp. 238–44.

17. Edgar H. Schein, *Process Consultation: Its Role in Organizational Development* (Reading, Mass.: Addison-Wesley, 1969).

18. James F. Engel and Roger D. Blackwell, *Consumer Behavior*, 4th ed. (New York: Dryden, 1982), pp. 416–42.

19. Gerald Zaltman and Melanie Wallendorf, *Consumer Behavior: Basic Findings and Management Implications* (New York: John Wiley & Sons, 1983), pp. 550–51.

20. Engel and Blackwell, *Consumer Behavior*, p. 444.

21. Ibid., p. 418.

22. Edward E. Lawler, III, *Motivation in Work Organizations* (Monterey, Calif.: Brooks/Cole, 1973).

23. D. McClelland and D.H. Burnham, "Power Is the Great Motivator," *Harvard Business Review* (March-April 1976), pp. 100–10.

24. David C. McClelland, *The Achieving Society* (New York: Van Nostrand Reinhold, 1961).

25. John B. Miner, "Twenty Years of Research on Role Motivation Theory," *Personnel Psychology*, Vol. 31 (1978), pp. 739–60.

26. Ralph Stogdill, *Handbook of Leadership: A Survey of Theory and Research* (New York: Free Press, 1974).

27. Bass, *Organizational Decision Making*, p. 83.

28. McClelland, *Achieving Society*.

29. Kogan and Wallach, *Risk Taking*, p. 187.

30. Bass, *Organizational Decision Making*, p. 88.

31. P. Slovic, R. Fischhoff, and S. Lichtenstein, "Behavioral Decision Theory," *Annual Review of Psychology*, Vol. 28 (1977), pp. 1–39.

32. Victor H. Vroom and Bernard Pahl, "Relationship between Age and Risk Taking among Managers," *Journal of Applied Psychology*, Vol. 55, No. 5 (1971), pp. 399–405.

33. S. Streufert, "Complex Military Decision Making," *Naval Research Review*, Vol. 23 (1978), pp. 12–19.

34. Bass, *Organizational Decision Making*, p. 184.

35. J.E. Thompson and A.L. Carsrud, "The Effects of Experimentally Induced Illusions of Invulnerability and Vulnerability in Decisional Risk Taking in Triads," *Journal of Social Psychology*, Vol. 100 (1976), pp. 263–67.

36. Bass, *Organizational Decision Making*, p. 90.

37. Vroom and Pahl, "Relationship," p. 400.

38. George W. England, "Managers and Their Value Systems: A Five-Country Comparative Study," *Columbia Journal of World Business* (Summer 1978).

39. Yukl, *Leadership*, p. 84; and Warren H. Schmidt and Barry Z. Posner, *Managerial Values and Expectations: The Silent Power in Personal and Organizational Life* (New York: American Management Association, 1982).

40. Paul R. Lawrence and Jay W. Lorsch, *Organization and Environment* (Homewood, Ill.: Richard D. Irwin, 1969).

41. George C. Homan, *Social Behavior: Its Elementary Forms* (New York: Harcourt Brace Jovanovich, 1961).

42. Thomas J. Peters and Robert H. Waterman, Jr., *In Search of Excellence* (New York: Harper & Row, 1982); and Kanter, *Change Masters*.

7

The Impact of Innovation Decisions

Innovation decisions are a form of managerial control. Regardless of whether the choice is to continue or to end the innovation process, it discernably affects at least part of the organization. Managers who understand what tends to tighten or loosen their control of innovation, and who can anticipate some of the potential consequences of their use of control should be equipped to approach the challenge of making good decisions about innovation.

Tight control of innovation occurs when organizational objectives are translated into specific, often quantitative, performance standards that new administrative systems, products, or production processes must promise to meet. The lower the hierarchical level to which these standards are communicated, the tighter control is. The earlier in the innovation process decisions applying these standards are made to continue or to stop, the tighter the managerial control.

Innovation is loosely controlled when its promised performance criteria are not closely related to organizational objectives and/or when they are neither preestablished nor particularly quantitative. Even if organizational goals are translated into quantitative hurdles, when only top management knows about them, control of innovation is fairly loose. Finally, the later in the innovation process economics-based decisions are made to continue or to stop, the looser is managerial control.

Many organizations use both types of control. Two common approaches to controlling innovation via successive economic evaluations are to begin with tight control and become progressively looser or to begin with loose control and become progressively tighter. In the first approach to selecting innovations, new things are evaluated in their earliest stages by lower levels of management that have the greatest technical knowledge about them. If numerical criteria are applied at these early developmental stages, it is likely that the more radical innovations will be unable to meet these criteria and will, therefore, be rejected.

Under these circumstances, then, more evolutionary innovations promising to meet criteria at their early stages will be chosen. As they develop, it becomes more and more likely that they will continue to be approved by successively higher levels of management. At the top of the hierarchy, all innovations are approved because the critical decisions have already been made. Control loosens as innovation decisions move upward through the hierarchy and as the innovation's development progresses. Furthermore, if organizational goals are known by all and standards are adhered to by everyone because they are enforced, it becomes unlikely that anything that does not meet standards will be proposed. Consequently, anything that is radically new is unlikely to be put forward even at the earliest phase.

For instance, in semiconductor company C (the least innovative division in the sample studied as the basis for this book), applications engineers work closely with marketing managers and learn about microelectronics group goals from them. While circuit and process designers are only informally aware of these goals, they are encouraged to go in a particular direction on a design that may promise to capture a 20 percent market share, for example. The clarity with which goals are communicated is indicated by the fact that new-product proposals are never rejected due to financial inadequacy. The director of product planning noted, "We're all aware of our financial situation, so no one submits anything that would strain it."

In semiconductor company A, testimony to the clarity with which new-product goals are communicated to researchers is the fact that few new-item proposals are rejected by top divisional management due to financial inadequacy. The general manager explained this by saying that financial objectives are known to all from the start. By contrast, at company B (the most innovative division because of the revolutionary new device it was introducing at the time of this analysis), only the co-managers of the laboratory are told about the preestablished net return on assets, sales, and earnings goals. The bench engineers may hear rumors about them, but they are not formally told. Between 10 and 20 percent of new-product proposals submitted are ultimately rejected due to financial inadequacy.

At pharmaceuticals company G, by industry reputation the least innovative of that subsample, new products must promise to meet fixed, preestablished hurdles before they are approved for market introduction. The project leaders are the main channel through which goals are communicated. The marketing people for the pharmaceuticals group provide all commercial data to the project leaders. Another 5 percent of proposals were rejected due to financial inadequacy before they were submitted to the Food and Drug Administration for review.

At company E (a division with more revolutionary drugs to its credit), the progression is similar except that at the final stage, no products are rejected as they are in company G. Between 50 and 75 percent of new drug proposals are rejected due to financial inadequacy when they reach the product candidate stage at which critical decisions are made. Bench scientists are not aware of commercial criteria that must be met, however.

In the second approach to selecting innovations (which begins with loose control but ends with tight control), economic decisions are made at later stages of the innovation process by managers at higher levels in the organizational hierarchy. Economic performance criteria are not communicated to those who initiate the innovations. For instance, at drug company D (by industry reputation the most innovative of the entire sample), at the first major screen, the rejection rate is less than 1 percent, meaning that out of 200 ideas, only one is rejected. Although management could not provide a percentage rejection rate at the next screen, it appears that financial criteria are not applied until the first batch of the compound is tested, a point that comes much later in development. Only the president of the laboratory is told what the corporation's preestablished return on investment, market share, and other commercial goals are. No effort is made to communicate them to the people doing research.

According to the laboratory's president, the economics of a new compound are not considered at the early stages of its development because the scientists do not know if they have the proper entity at all and no time has yet been devoted to discovering the process issues of how the compound will be made. Sales estimates cannot be done because there are too many unknown factors. Furthermore, the president feels that estimating at this phase can actually be counterproductive because it stifles creativity. Only after clinical testing do a compound's commercial features become important, as market research and financial people work on its projected costs.

In most of these divisions, both tight and loose control are used. Each type has its good and bad points. The purpose of this discussion is not to advocate either, but rather to present decision makers with the range of degrees of control and some possible consequences so that they can best approach their own organizational situations.

Proportion of Innovations Selected

One way of gauging the overall degree of control exerted by innovation decisions is the proportion of new things that are actually selected for further development and implementation of the total that are proposed. In general, the lower the proportion of innovations accepted for implementation, the tighter the control exerted and vice versa.

For example, it appears that tight control is exerted over most consumer product innovation. Some studies have found that only between 2 and 5 percent of new-product concepts survive the development and evaluation process. Conversely, the rejection rate is between 95 and 98 percent. The figures do vary, however, depending upon definitions of terms. It may also depend importantly upon the type of industry.[1] In fact, data from the semiconductor and ethical pharmaceutical industries, in which innovation is the driving force behind survival and growth, indicate a higher survival rate of new products.

Table 7-1 compares rejection rates at three important points in new semi-

Table 7-1
Comparative Rejection Rates for New Products

	Phase		
Company	*Prefeasibility*	*Prototype*	*Preintroduction*
Semiconductor			
A	NA	5%	5%
B	50%	10	0
C	NA	< 5	5
Pharmaceuticals			
D	.005%(1/200)	NA	< 1
E	60	20	0
F	25	15	5
G	60	20	5

Note: NA = not available.

conductor and pharmaceutical products' development. In all but one company, the highest rate of rejection occurred at the end of what has been termed the prefeasibility phase. It is at this point in many industries that formal proposals for significantly more funding are submitted in order to make a prototype or first batch for further testing. The reason is the cost of equipment and facilities needed to make this initial product—up to $100,000 in company B, for instance. In three out of the seven companies, the rejection rate was between 50 and 60 percent, implying a survival rate of between 40 and 50 percent at the first economic evaluation point.

Either during attempts to make their prototypes or after they were tested with prospective users, each company dropped even more products, but a smaller percentage. In the semiconductor firms, the percentages were smaller than those in the drug firms, implying that the earliest screen may be the finest or most difficult to penetrate. In two of the drug companies, another 20 percent were dropped after clinical testing—a fairly high percentage. Even after market or clinical testing, four of the seven companies rejected about 5 percent of their new products and never introduced them.

Based on the data in table 7-1, we can conclude that in company B, an average of 45 percent of ideas made it to product introduction; in company E the proportion of new ideas introduced was 32 percent; in company F, 60 percent; and in company G, 30 percent. The lower the percentage of introductions, the tighter was the evaluation system.

Also, the earlier the more proposals were rejected, the tighter the system. We can infer, for example, that if only 5 percent of proposals were rejected in the last two phases in companies A and C, then most were rejected at the first phase in the process, indicating tight managerial control. Company D, however, rejected most proposals at a later stage of development, revealing looser managerial control in the evaluation system.

Proportion of Funded Innovations That Succeed

Do tight evaluation systems prevent new-product or other kinds of innovation from failing? Again referring to the semiconductor and pharmaceuticals companies sampled, table 7–2 presents comparative data about self-reported success rates in introducing new products.

This table shows that between 20 and 30 percent of all new-product introductions failed in this sample. Because of its small size, it is difficult to identify any relationship between tightness of the evaluation system and failure rate. Thus, it is not clear whether tighter systems prevent failure or not. In fact, in the semiconductor subsample, although company A's system was tighter than company B's, both had an average failure rate over ten years' time of 25 percent.

In the pharmaceuticals sample, on the other hand, company F's evaluation system, which was relatively loose in that 60 percent of new ideas were introduced to the market, seemed to produce a failure rate of 30 percent, while company G's system, which only permitted 30 percent of new ideas to be introduced, generated a failure rate of 20 percent. It may be that the relationship between exerting control and success rates only holds in certain industries.

Other studies also have shown that the average new-product failure rate is 25 percent for industrial products. It is higher for consumer products: 30 to 35 percent.[2] While these figures may not seem to be terribly high, the actual costs of failure are high enough to constitute substantial downside risk in new-product decision making.

For instance, in semiconductor company A, the minimum development cost of a new product requiring new production technology is $1 million. Semicon-

Table 7–2
New-Product–Introduction Success Rates

Semiconductor Company	(10-year average)
A	75%
B	75
C	NA
Pharmaceutical Company	
D	NA
E	75
F	70
G	80

NA = not available.

ductor company B, which was just about to introduce a radically new device at the time of the survey, constructed a new facility for it at a cost of at least $30 million. In this division, new-product project operating costs averaged $438,000 annually. In pharmaceuticals company D, the cost and length of time required to develop a given new product were close to the industry average of $55 million over eight to ten years.

Less is known about proposal rejection rates and success rates in adopting innovation than in generating new things.[3] Instead, the literature focusses upon how long it takes for specific new products, technologies, and nontechnical knowledge to diffuse throughout a society. The less time it takes and the more widely diffused it is, presumably the more innovative the society. There is some indication that the rate of innovation adoption is increasing over time.[4]

Rejecting Innovation

One inevitable outcome of the selection phase of innovation is that some proposals are rejected. Joseph Bower has observed four ways of doing so. The decision maker may place higher priority on the proposer's other activities and structure the proposer's incentives or job so that the project is dropped. Another technique is to ask questions requiring further study, thereby indefinitely postponing the project. Alternatively, the proposer can be told that the timing isn't right for the project. Finally, ignoring the request for a proposal review can serve as a pocket veto. According to Bower, these techniques are generally used when the reasons for rejecting the new idea are not entirely based upon the nature of the innovation itself, but rather upon political considerations.[5]

Regardless of the reasons for the rejection, it can be a problem for decision makers because it may arouse feelings that can negatively affect innovators' motivation and job performance. There are at least two principal reasons for innovators to react negatively: (1) the belief that the rejection wasted their time, effort, money, and other resources, and (2) the belief that the rejection represents failure to perform their jobs adequately.

Innovators' needs are frustrated by rejection, and the frustration can take a variety of forms, including anger.[6] Other feelings (such as disappointment, embarrassment, resentment, guilt, reduced self-esteem, anxiety about job security in the company and/or anxiety about competence in one's industry, profession, or discipline) may not be expressed directly. In fact, they may be carefully hidden and denied, even to the person having them.

There are at least two approaches that can be taken to minimize negative reactions to rejected innovations. One approach directs the manager's efforts at modifying innovators' perceptions. The manager can make it clear that whatever went into developing the new thing was not wasted. A list should be made of all the benefits that the company has derived from developing the innovation, such as training personnel, obtaining new information about a technology or market, and clarifying corporate strategy.

One such benefit worthy of highlighting is the creation of a file of previously rejected innovations that can be periodically reexamined. As external factors (such as technological advances, competition, market demand, and government regulations) change, what is viewed as a reject in the present could well become highly desirable in the future.[7] Managers should try to minimize the perception that a rejected innovation represents a failure on the part of anyone who worked to develop it. One way of putting distance between the reject and its developers is to point out the vast number of unpredictable, uncontrollable factors that are inherent in any kind of innovation.

Another approach to dealing with negative reactions to rejection is to confront the emotions that are aroused. Many people are conditioned not to express emotions, especially at work. Few people are likely to go into a manager's office to cry on his or her shoulder or vent their anger. If a manager suspects that some members of the rejected innovation's team are harboring negative feelings, and if he or she feels able to nonjudgmentally listen to and accept these feelings, then the manager should consider initiating a conversation with each affected individual.[8] One of the best ways to manage emotions is to allow them to be expressed. Under the right circumstances, a one-to-one conversation can be just the kind of safety valve that will prevent delayed explosions or alienation.

An option for structuring the opportunity to express negative feelings is to institute the practice of conducting individual postproject interviews with key members of every rejected innovation's development process. The ostensible purpose for such meetings would be to create a "What did we learn from this?" list. The interviews could be conducted by senior members of the company's staff, such as a planning or human resource development manager. Whoever this interviewer is, he or she should be aware of the dual purpose of the interview and be skilled in the techniques of nonjudgmental listening.

These suggestions for rejecting innovation may be applied at any point in the development process. If a new idea is scrapped after the feasibility-testing stage, the same perceptions of waste and failure and the same negative feelings may occur. The likelihood of their occurrence and their intensity usually increase, however, with the degree of development a project has reached by the time of its rejection. Thus, the later in the development process that rejection occurs, the more necessary it is for the manager to do something about the problem.

One of the primary reasons for discussing options for managing rejection is to make it easier for managers to continue to develop innovations as far as possible before rejecting them. In so doing, more information is gathered, thereby improving the decision that is made. The chance of making the common error of giving up too soon on what turns out to be a lucrative innovation can be minimized.

For example, compact disk players, which use a revolutionary technology involving lasers to produce sounds and pictures from small plastic disks, were ultimately rejected as new products by RCA and Zenith Electronics. Despite the fact that both firms had invested millions of dollars in research to develop the technology during the middle 1970s, by the end of the decade, their managements decided that the projects were too risky. RCA lost $500 million trying unsuccessfully to market videodisks. Zenith never introduced them. Sony of Japan, however, persevered, and by the mid-1980s, led the competition in this market. N.V. Phillips, the Dutch electronics firm, originated much of the technology and convinced Sony to join it in commercializing the innovation.[9]

Too often, new ideas are rejected too soon because, as in this example, the costs associated with rejecting them at a later phase are believed to be too high.[10] One of the intangible costs is the repercussions on morale that late rejections can have. By knowing what to do to alleviate the pain associated with late rejections, however, a manager gains more freedom to scrap a new project at the final phase if necessary, despite the organizational momentum that probably has built up in support of it.

Implementing Innovation: An Overview of Key Issues

If a decision is made to allocate significant resources for bringing something new to fruition, the innovation process becomes one of implementation. This term is used very broadly here to apply to both the generation and adoption of new products, services, processes, and administrative systems. It is also broad enough to encompass the more traditional labels that are used to describe the subphases of the various forms of innovation.

A case in point is the new product/service development process, which typically uses the term *commercialization* to describe how an innovation is first made in sufficient quantities (pilot production) for some form of testing with users (field or market testing), refined, reevaluated, and finally introduced to the market. Despite the fact that these steps are particular to new-product or -service development, all of them are taken for the ultimate purpose of making the new thing part of the organization's ongoing business.

Implementation in general, then, is the process by which innovating organizations incorporate anything new into their routine functioning. Implementation requires the completion of several tasks that correspond loosely to the subphases through which a new product or service passes. These tasks are: to mobilize financial and human resources; to try out and adjust the innovation and to make a final decision about whether or not to complete the process; and, if it is completed, to formally announce the completion of the innovation outside of the immediate organization.

The implementation phases of innovation differ from the preselection phases (strategy formulation, conceptualization, feasibility-testing, and selling the new idea). The primary difference is that, unless they have initiated the new thing, managers at all levels become more active in the innovation process during implementation. In general, management can and often should exert more control and use more formal devices to do so once it has committed itself to having the innovation, whatever it is. Even if top management gets the idea for an innovation and hands it down to lower levels for implementation, it should continue to play an active role to insure that the innovation meets its intended goals and remains within organizational constraints.

The main reason for increased or continued managerial control when implementing new things is that it is widely acknowledged that the costs of innovation (especially for new products or processes requiring new equipment and facilities) escalate dramatically during this phase. For instance, over the eight years that it took to develop Mylar polyester film, the average annual research expenditure for the first four years was $400,000. Technical manpower utilization during this time averaged eight man-years. During the last four years of development, however, average annual expenditures increased fourfold, while technical manpower utilization rose to an annual average of thirty-eight man-years.[11]

Many managers recognize that successfully executing their responsibilities to control costs, meet deadlines, and see that the innovation delivers on its promises is much more difficult than generating new ideas and convincing others of their worth. Implementing innovation raises a number of implicit issues of which general managers should be well aware because they can be the source of problems that needlessly increase an innovation's demand on organizations' human and financial resources or, more seriously, cause it to fail altogether.

These issues fall into three closely related categories: technical, business, and organizational. Indeed, some innovation scholars are calling for a formally defined discipline of implementation in order to better understand why so many problems and failures occur at this phase of the innovation process and what can be done to improve its management.[12]

Technical Implementation Issues

The innovation itself (its nature, how it works, and what it requires in order to work properly) is the source of technical issues during implementation. Can and does the new thing function as it is intended to do under realistic conditions? These conditions can be physical factors (such as temperature, moisture, vibration, and light) or demand factors (such as quantity, quality, and rate of production).

Other questions also present themselves. Are the necessary trained personnel, supplies, equipment, and facilities available and reliable? Does the innovation actually fit with existing systems or technology as it was expected to do?

Are there any unanticipated side effects or problems caused by using the new thing? Can management—and does it want to—accommodate or solve these unanticipated consequences?

A good example of technical implementation issues that have become problems is the adoption of automated manufacturing processes by the U.S. automobile industry. In some plants, robots, cameras, and lasers may be idle for months because problems in the software controlling them must be solved and because—despite months of training—workers are still unable to operate the sophisticated equipment correctly.

In some instances, new products must be modified in less than desirable ways because the original design cannot be accommodated by the new production equipment. One major consequence of all of these problems is that new-product launches have been delayed. Ford Motor Company's 1986 Taurus and Sable models were three months late, for instance.[13]

Business Implementation Issues

In actually carrying out an innovation, its intended purpose or set of objectives must be kept in mind. One approach to measuring the business success of an innovation uses three indicators: productivity increase, attainment of other kinds of benefits, in addition to productivity increases (such as more flexibility), and transformation of these benefits into competitive market advantage.[14]

Specific questions raised as the innovation progresses toward completion, then, include: Do the results of tests, trial usage, and other forms of data collection corroborate the original proposal's estimates or promises of the innovation's performance? Are the goals and benefits achieved in the degree and kind anticipated or not? What are the unexpected benefits or disadvantages? Do we want to tolerate these disadvantages? Can we afford them?

The computer industry's move toward linking existing incompatible office personal computers highlights some of the problems that can emerge from the issues surrounding whether or not innovations actually deliver their promised benefits. In terms of generating the new networks (which consist of coaxial cable, insertable circuit cards, and software), companies such as Xerox, Digital Equipment Corp., Intel, and IBM have found that in addition to the technical difficulties of producing such technology, its costs are higher than expected. Additionally, existing networks seem to worsen problems that they were intended to solve, such as translation of one computer's data into a form usable by others, manual exchange of floppy diskettes, and the logistical placement of cabling.[15]

From the perspective of some companies adopting such networks, such as American Express and Arthur Andersen, it is not yet clear that having them will simplify data storage and access needed for administrative duties, make possible new services, and enhance competitive position. Some data must be kept confidential within units, and linking together all units' PCs can make it difficult to maintain secrecy, for example.[16]

Organizational Implementation Issues

Any human organization, whether it is a group of five people or a multinational corporation, may be considered to be a system of interconnecting units (departments, divisions, groups, or hierarchical levels) such that a change in one part causes some sort of change in another part or parts. If the term innovation is substituted for change, the following hypotheses can be made.

In general, the more radical the innovation in one part of the organizational system, the greater the number of other parts of the system that are likely to be affected and required to change also whether they want to or not. Thus, the likelihood of conflict between parts of the organization increases.

Because of the heightened chance of friction, the more radical the innovation and the more parts of the system are affected, the longer it is likely to take for the innovation to be implemented or for a new equilibrium to be achieved. Conversely, the less new an innovation in one part of the organizational system, the fewer the number of other parts of the system that are likely to be affected and required to change also. Friction is less likely to occur. Therefore, the less time it is likely to take for the innovation to be implemented.

As the tasks of implementation are undertaken, the systems nature of organizations becomes more acutely apparent than at any earlier point in the innovation process. Once management selects an innovation, people, money, materials, equipment, and/or facilities from a wide range of departments may have to be committed to it as the first step in making it a lasting reality in the organization.

As one manufacturing vice president in the bedding industry noted, however, "getting people to go along" can be the most difficult part of the entire innovation process. In many cases, the necessary resources are controlled by individuals and groups outside of the domain of an innovation's initiators and sponsors. Although the managers with authority to approve something new may have been sold on the idea, these other parties may not have been sold yet. A program manager in one innovative high technology firm likened the attitude of some people toward implementing an innovation to that of raising a child. "When it stops lying there and being cute, then what do we do with it? Everybody says, 'Give me a kid with no diapers and a college education!'"

Among the questions that general management must consider about the organizational aspects of implementing all kinds of innovations are: How effective is communication, coordination, and cooperation among both the vertical and horizontal units of our organization?[17] Where is the most resistance to the new thing likely to occur? What are the real reasons for this resistance? Can we, and do we want to, take action to remove these objections? Regardless of general management's support for something new, there may be many legitimate reasons for the people who must actually do the work to be reluctant to make time in their schedules, expend extra effort on the project, or part with some of their needed people, materials, or space. Quite often, these reasons stem from the three sets of implementation issues that have been presented here. Resistance, therefore, can be a very useful warning signal of deeper problems that can be headed off or taken care of early enough to prevent them from causing the innovation's demise.

Despite its utility as a warning device, however, resistance is commonly viewed by managers as a problem itself. It is very easy to believe that "you can't teach an old dog new tricks" and that human nature is inherently against change. Because of this widely held attitude, and the pervasiveness and importance to successful implementation of organizational resistance, the next section analyzes such resistance in more depth.

Organizational Resistance to the Outcomes of Innovation Decisions: Threat or Opportunity?

Regardless of whether something new is selected or rejected, it is likely that someone somewhere in the organization will disagree with the decision. Such disagreement is natural and inevitable given the diversity of people and their needs, goals, and interests. Disagreement with a decision does not always mean refusal to comply with it, but when it does, resistance occurs.

Under what conditions do innovation decisions lead to resistance? When individuals perceive such decisions as frustrating the fulfillment of their needs by thwarting goal achievement or punishing them in some way, they will be reluctant to go along with an innovation. Similarly, when organizational groups, such as departments, preceive that an innovation harms them in some way more than it helps them, they will be resistant.[18]

Something new can pose "harm" if it is seen to take away or reduce something valued. This "something" can be autonomy, authority, prestige, self-esteem, money, informal influence, or any other tangible or intangible reward that is currently motivating to the individual or group.

For example, implementing an innovative performance evaluation system may be strongly resisted by lower-level managers if it reduces their autonomy to hire, evaluate, and promote their own employees. A new piece of equipment that speeds up production may also prevent workers from socializing with each other as they were happy to do, thereby causing resistance to it. Salespeople may resist testing or selling a new product if doing so takes away from their time to make normal sales quotas and they are not compensated in some way for making what they view to be an extra effort.

Few organizational members have the power to absolutely refuse to go along with an innovation decision made by top management. Outright insubordination is generally not tolerated. Therefore, in most instances, resistance takes on the appearance of more benign behaviors that can be attributed to other causes. For instance, salespeople who do not want to test a new product somehow never get time in their calls to bring up the new item. People keep forgetting new procedures or claim that they are too difficult to learn.

The intended, albeit generally unconscious, message to management is that the person is at fault rather than the new thing, but that the fault is beyond their control. Resistant people often say that they simply cannot get themselves motivated to do the new thing, whatever it is, and they do not know why. They would like to, but they just cannot do it. When presented with such an attitude, it is difficult for managers to blame those having it with deliberate obstruction or sabotage of the innovation. After all, they *are* making an attempt, are they not?

It is also often difficult for management to distinguish whether the resistance is the cause or the symptom of the implementation problem, and what that basic problem is. A good example is the autoworkers who do not use the new automated equipment in their factories of the future. Are they simply blaming its sophistication because they have other reasons for not wanting to automate the plants? Or is this really a technical implementation problem, that is, is the equipment itself too complex and unreliable? Or, is this an organizational problem, that is, a conflict between labor's and management's long-term views of labor's role in producing cars?

While it could be said that it does not matter which is the cause and which is the symptom, in reality it does matter, because much time and money could be spent modifying the equipment to make it easier to use only to have workers blame something else for their inability to make it operate properly. Similarly, management could make unnecessary concessions to protect job security in labor contracts, only to find that it was, in fact, the equipment's complexity that kept workers from using it to its best advantage.

Although much resistance to innovation can stem from implementation issues, it can also come from individuals' or groups' anger about issues unrelated or indirectly related to the new thing. It then becomes a lightning rod that attracts any bad feelings people have about the innovation's implementers, the decision maker, or the organization in general. Because it is likely to be kept hidden, such resistance is difficult for managers to deal with directly. In such cases, calling in a professional organizational consultant to diagnose the situation and make recommendations may be necessary.

The points being made here are (1) that resistance to innovation generally has a hidden cause that is valid from the point of view of the resistant individual or group and (2) that it is in management's best interest to try to sort out what this cause, or set of causes, is so that action can be taken to reduce the resistance.

Notice that the term *reduce* rather than *overcome* is used. Innovations can be, and all too often are, forced through organizations despite resistance, especially when top management has initiated them or strongly committed itself to them.

Whether or not such forced innovations last or live up to their potential for improvement, however, is often a matter of members' attitudes toward them. Feelings of frustration, opposition, resentment, and/or being disenfranchised as a result of the innovation process can slow its progress and undermine its success. Therefore, *how* the innovation is implemented is critically important.

Contrary to what many managers think, most individuals are not inherently against change. In fact, many people seek change if they see it as representing an improvement in their situation or in themselves. The key to predicting whether an individual will welcome or resist something new is to know whether or not that individual perceives it to be helpful or harmful to him or her.[19]

Of course, if individuals are directly asked why they have a particular attitude toward something new, they may not be able to tell you because they have not articulated to themselves just what about this new thing affects their self-interest, they may not have articulated what their self-interest is, or they may be reluctant to reveal what their self-interest is. Nonetheless, most people appreciate management's showing an interest in their opinions and concerns about something new and taking action upon their comments.

General managers can do much to set the tone for carrying out innovation. Their sensitivity to the potential for resistance and their willingness to learn its causes and to do something about them can facilitate the implementation part of the process. More specifically, general managers are in a position to design the procedures and channels by which innovation is carried out. The next chapter considers design options that can prevent or minimize some of the implementation problems identified thus far.

Notes

1. C. Merle Crawford, *New Products Management* (Homewood, Ill.: Richard D. Irwin, 1983), p. 26.

2. Crawford, *New Products*, pp. 26–28.

3. C.A. Voss, "Research Notes: The Need for a Field of Study of Implementation of Innovations," *Journal of Product Innovation Management*, Vol. 2, No. 4 (December 1985), pp. 266–71.

4. Richard Olshavsky, "Time and the Rate of Adoption of Innovation," *Journal of Consumer Research* (March 1980), pp. 425–28.

5. Joseph L. Bower, *Managing the Resource Allocation Process: A Study of Corporate Planning and Investment* (Homewood, Ill.: Richard D. Irwin, 1970), p. 59.

6. The ideas on managing rejection in this paragraph and in the following section are reprinted from my earlier work, *How to Manage the New Product Development Process*,

pp. 137–38, 140. (© 1982, American Management Association, New York. All rights reserved.)

7. Thomas C. Treeger, "Where Product Development Gets into Trouble," in *Managing Advancing Technology*, Vol. I, edited by the staff of *Innovation Magazine* (New York: AMACOM, 1972), pp. 151–62.

8. For a detailed description of the nonjudgmental listening technique called "active listening," see Carl B. Rogers and Richard E. Farson, "Acting Listening," in *Effective Behavior in Organizations*, 2nd ed., Allan R. Cohen et al. (eds.) (Homewood, Ill.: Richard D. Irwin, 1980), pp. 227–91.

9. E.S. Browning, "Sony's Perserverance Helped It Win Market for Mini-CD Players," *Wall Street Journal*, February 27, 1986, p.1.

10. Treeger, "Trouble," p. 159.

11. Edwin A. Gee and Chaplin Tyler, *Managing Innovation* (New York: John Wiley, 1976), p. 81.

12. Voss, "Research Notes," pp. 268, 270.

13. Amal Nag, "Auto Makers Discover 'Factory of the Future' Is Headache Just Now," *Wall Street Journal*, May 13, 1986, p. 1.

14. Voss, "Research Notes," p. 268.

15. Dennis Kneale, "Linking of Office PCs Is Coming, but Plenty of Obstacles Remain," *Wall Street Journal*, January 28, 1986, p. 1.

16. Kneale, "Linking," p. 22.

17. For in-depth analyses and recommendations for solving problems in these areas, see Lori A. Fidler and J. David Johnson, "Communication and Innovation Implementation," *Academy of Management Review*, Vol. 9, No. 4 (October 1984), pp. 704–11; Dorothy Leonard-Barton and William A. Kraus, "Implementing New Technology," *Harvard Business Review*, Vol. 63, No. 6 (November-December 1985), pp. 102–10; and Hirotaka Takeuchi and Ikujiro Nonaka, "The New New Product Development Game," *Harvard Business Review*, Vol. 64, No. 1 (January-February 1986), pp. 137–46.

18. Walter Sikes, "Some Principles of Personal and Organizational Change," *NTL (National Training Laboratories) Connections* (March 1985), pp. 5–6.

19. Paul R. Lawrence, "How to Deal with Resistance to Change," *Harvard Business Review* (January-February 1969), HBR Classic Reprint No. 69107.

8

Mobilizing Resources for Innovation

General managers are responsible for simultaneously insuring that innovations get what they need from the organization while preventing new things from jeopardizing the organization's ongoing health by making unreasonable demands of it. Consequently, they must control the way in which financial and human resources are used to bring to fruition new ideas.

To achieve this balance, general managers design procedures, structures, and systems for budgeting money and organizing personnel. Such designs should permit them to monitor innovations' performance as it unfolds during implementation, evaluate it, and determine whether or not previous decisions to innovate should be reversed. The purpose of this chapter is to analyze some design aspects of budgeting and organizing for innovation that are related to the implementation issues outlined in chapter 7. This analysis is meant to help general managers to minimize the seemingly inevitable technical, business, and organizational problems that plague the implementation phase.

Budgeting for Innovation

General managers typically review and negotiate budget amounts that are proposed by innovations' originators, primary sponsors, or project managers. They also interpret deviations from expected expenditures and call for adjustments as necessary. Managers use the information produced by a budget to aid in their continued decision making about whether or not to finalize the innovation.

In order to carry out this role, however, general management usually relies upon the accounting function. Accountants are also important during the proposal preparation phase of innovation because they typically provide estimates about costs, cash flow projections, and calculations such as the innovation's expected return on investment. In some firms, they may use sophisticated models to perform risk analyses. Additionally, many firms expect the accounting function to play a watchdog role either as a voice of caution and restraint in the innovation selection phase or as the monitor in the implementation phase.

Accounting groups are able to take on this role because they have the necessary information and are generally more objective about the new thing, unless, of course, they are trying to do something new themselves, such as automate or implement new methods. They are responsible for collecting actual cost data, organizing them into reports, and returning them to the appropriate managers for their interpretation and action, if necessary.

A number of common problems have been identified, however, in the general management–accounting relationship as it concerns innovation. One such problem is that accountants often provide general managers with raw figures but too little analysis, such as sensitivity analysis and comparisons to industry norms or organizational objectives. Another problem is that accounting departments may not be cooperative in providing information needed for decision making in a timely way, or they may not provide it at all. A pronouncement that the project costs too much may be made instead, without supporting evidence.[1]

General managers who accept cost estimates as precise and make poor decisions based solely on them often blame accountants for these estimates. Accountants counter that general management is responsible for the interpretation and use of estimates. They suggest asking for ranges that could serve as reminders of the estimates' imprecision. Finally, some general managers believe that accountants generate more unsolicited reports than are necessary, thereby diluting the impact of those that are really important.[2]

The Relationship between Budget and Innovation Decisions

An innovation's preliminary budget is actually contained in its formal funding proposal because the estimates of resources needed for continued adoption or development are presented in it. Nonetheless, in some organizations, the general budget cycle and innovation decisions are separate from each other. The following three aspects of the relationship between budget and innovation decisions are worth considering because they are related to technical, business, or organizational problems in implementing innovations.

Type of Budget Required by the Approved Innovation. In their earliest phases, most innovations' primary costs appear in operating budgets as innovators' salaries and perhaps travel expenses for attendance at conferences, trade shows, and other types of professional or industry gatherings where ideas can be exchanged. There may be consultants' fees or costs of conducting concept tests, as described in chapter 4 on reality testing, but it is unlikely that additional equipment, facilities, or permanent personnel will be needed. Since innovators' salaries, benefits, and expenses would have to be paid anyway at the earliest phases of innovation, it is generally considered not worth the effort required to have distinct innovation project operating budgets.

Innovation decisions that intersect with capital budgeting decisions differ from those intersecting only with operating budgeting decisions in a number of ways. Innovations requiring capital investment are often fewer in number in any year's budget, but longer-term in nature. The actual amount of funding tends to be greater for capital investments than for operating expenditures, with the exception of advertising expenses. Furthermore, it is more likely that capital budgets must be approved by a firm's board of directors.

For all of these reasons, innovations requiring capital investment are more visible and represent higher stakes than do those only requiring operating funds. Accountability for them may be clearer and at higher levels of the organization. The financial and career costs of failure may well be perceived to be much greater. Even though an innovation may be approved to continue by management in one decision process, it is conceivable that when it becomes part of the normal capital budgeting cycle, the decision may shift somewhat to allocate less money than the proposal had originally requested.

In some instances, capital investment's risks may be incurred by managers in units that did not come up with the new idea in the first place. Indeed, it is often the production, manufacturing, or operations function of the organization that takes primary responsibility for installing new equipment and facilities requested initially by either the marketing, engineering, or accounting functions. It is easy to see, then, how the organizational units most affected by capital investment and most responsible for insuring that it is implemented successfully may resent innovations as sources of more work and little immediate reward.

Given these difficulties, some proposers of innovation may consciously try to avoid having to ask for capital by making do with existing facilities and equipment. On the other hand, some companies' management refuses to make additional investments until the capacity of all existing facilities is completely utilized. Regardless of the reasons for it, this practice can lead to unnecessary technical problems in implementing the innovation. Additionally, more radical innovations of all kinds are much more likely to require new capital, and aversion to making such investments has long been recognized as one of the major inhibitors of revolutionary innovation.

As always, there is a bright side to capital budgeting for innovation. One positive aspect is that the visibility and rewards are great for managers who successfully bring new capital into the organization. Such innovation can be seen as a tremendous accomplishment and bettering of the company, and the responsible managers' careers often benefit considerably. Another positive feature is that the unit that takes responsibility for putting new capital into use becomes that much more powerful in the organization. Awareness of its relative indispensability to other units can be heightened at top levels, where such awareness counts in terms of getting future requests honored. Other units that benefit from successful implementation of new capital are more likely to return the favor at another time. Helping reluctant, risk-averse managers to see the positive aspects of investing capital for innovation is an important part of overcoming resistance to doing so.

The Timing of Budgeting Cycles and Innovation Decisions. The timing of innovation decisions as described in chapter 6 may or may not coincide with an organization's more general budgeting cycles. If, for example, a company sets its operating budget during October and November for the fiscal year starting in January, it may be possible for an innovation proposal to be submitted and acted upon during February, once the fiscal year has begun. On the other hand, some companies may require all innovation proposals to be submitted along with other kinds of requests made at the start of the general budgeting process.

The timing issue becomes important when there is some urgency to implement the innovation as soon as possible. Waiting for an approved new-product project to be officially budgeted may endanger its chances of being first to the market. In general, the more important it is for organizations to stay flexible and able to respond quickly and innovatively to environmental forces, the less sense it makes for innovation decisions to be collected and made only as part of normal budgeting cycles.

Innovations as Separate Line Items. Another aspect of the relationship between budgets and innovation decisions is whether or not any given innovation is considered to be a separate line item in the operating budget. The alternative is to consider the innovation as just one of a number of ongoing activities that are not specifically highlighted. For instance, one of the semiconductor divisions in the study reported in this book had abandoned the project accounting system for its new products, instead grouping them into programs.

The reason for this change was that each project could have as many as eight semiconductor devices being developed within it, and technical changes occurred constantly. One of the division's business unit managers had a greaseboard on the wall of his office, listing just one major project, and the myriad subprojects on it were updated almost hourly. Any cost accounting, therefore, could only be post hoc and could not be used for decision making. Division-level management believed that the overhead cost of tracking all projects was not justified.

Instead, a "blanket program budget" was used, and the business unit managers had discretion within it about where and how the money was spent. These innovations were evolutionary and relatively minor yet rapidly ongoing, making it unworkable to treat them as separate projects and correspondingly separate budget items. Indeed, there are many innovations of this nature that do not warrant project status, yet do require funding. Innovations in administrative systems that require additional money are generally included as budgeted overhead, for example.

There are at least two important reasons, however, to make a budget line item of an innovation of any kind, whether it is adoption of a new telecommunications system, design of a new faculty evaluation procedure, or development of a new service to transport children to and from their suburban homes to recreational facilities during the summer months. One reason is to set aside a certain amount of funding reserved exclusively for the new thing. An innovation project with its own budget is spotlighted and given legitimacy within the organization. The practice of separating out funding for innovation of all kinds, not just product development, has been used by such companies as Texas Instruments,[3] 3M, Eastman Kodak, and a leading bank.[4]

Another reason for highlighting an innovation in the budget is to provide information about its costs and progress toward completion. In fact, one of the functions of the trial phase, which comes next in the innovation process, can be to actually test out its costs and the rate at which it consumes resources. A separate budget permits this kind of control to be exerted.

Sources of Budgeted Amounts. In most instances, innovations in their earliest stages prior to being formally proposed for further development or implementation are funded from their initiating unit's operating budget. In these stages, they are relatively informal and not yet differentiated as projects or programs. It may be, however, that the initiating unit's management refuses to or cannot fund an innovation even at these early stages. In some organizations, a practice known as "tin cupping" occurs, in which innovators can approach managers outside of their own units for financial support.[5] In her study of innovative companies, Rosabeth Moss Kanter has found that budgetary discretion is decentralized to lower-level management, thereby permitting such cross-departmental funding of new things.[6]

Innovations that have formal project status as the result of general management approval generally derive their budget amounts from their proposals. For innovations that are undifferentiated as line items from the rest of the operating budget, however, the process by which operating budget amounts are established may have some impact on their continuation after formal approval. The way in which budget amounts are determined is usually a political process involving negotiations between levels of management.[7] In fact, some experts believe that budgeting should always be a participative process.[8]

Whether the approved innovation is funded by a cost center or a profit center can make a difference in what its budget for development looks like. For example, one survey found that some marketing departments responsible for new-product development were considered to be profit centers, in which managers' performance was judged on the basis of a "specified gross profit margin." The survey's authors concluded that this design did not stifle innovation because as long as the new products achieved profit margin goals, an unlimited amount of money could be spent on them. One respondent, in fact, pointed out that budgets could be changed "for any good reason," especially new-product development because it was the key to success.[9]

Other functional departments, however, such as manufacturing, human resource development, R&D, and accounting, may be considered to have responsibility for costs only. In this situation, funding for innovation may be much scarcer, unless the innovation can be directly linked to cost reduction itself.

In one semiconductor company, for example, the R&D lab was a separate cost center primarily funded by the division's operating groups such as bipolar or strategic operations. It also received money from other sources in the following percentages:

Corporate	3%
Semiconductor group	10
Integrated circuits division operating groups	80
Operations managers	5
Product managers	2
	100

Thus, the R&D laboratory was sponsored by the groups that were responsible for profitability. When their managers felt pressured to be profitable, they were reluctant to fund the lab; in a real crunch, some projects were abandoned. Furthermore, because this R&D lab was tied to the operating groups' profit and loss performance, it was necessary to have a tight budgeting system in place so that it could be used to change direction rapidly and to achieve short-term goals. The same situation also existed in one other semiconductor firm in the sample.

In many high technology companies, however, the R&D function may be a separate cost center funded by the corporate or next-lowest level (typically group or divisional). It is considered to be so important strategically that it does not feel the same kind of constraints in funding that are reflected in the above examples.

The Impact of Managerial Control

While budgeting is meant to force managers to plan ahead and set aside funds for future needs, contingencies arise that simply are not covered during the current period's budget. Where does the money come from to permit unplanned innovations or to solve unforeseen implementation problems? One option is for corporate, divisional, or group management to formally authorize interim contingency funds to be used. Of the seven companies studied, however, only two had a formal contingency fund. In four of the seven firms, formal requests were always needed to increase a budgeted project's allocation. And in the same proportion of firms, the budgeted amount for a project was never changed during the fiscal year.

Instead, the flexibility managers needed to provide financial resources for innovation came from slack that they had provided for themselves by overestimating their expenditures on certain items. With this slack, they could then juggle funds across accounts as necessary, while remaining within the expenditure limits already set. This practice is very common.[10]

In the most innovative of the semiconductor divisions, for example, the codirector of the R&D laboratory juggled funds between projects temporarily as the need arose. He had the autonomy to do this because two duplicate bookkeeping systems were used: one that kept track of engineering projects in order to see how cost effectively they were being carried out, and another more aggregate set of figures that constituted the departmental budget. Only total costs were reported to division level management.

Although some organizational theorists find such use of slack to be functional, if not harmless,[11] other experts believe it to be symptomatic of excessively tight control, a form of "gamesmanship." Although these methods do save managers the time and trouble of formally reapplying for additional funds, they have some drawbacks. Kenneth Merchant points that ultimately this practice can lead to poor operating performance because funds may not be allocated to areas needing them most. Furthermore, information provided to general management is distorted, providing an unreliable basis for decision making.[12]

Managerial control is exerted through budgets by periodically collecting information about an innovation's costs. Ongoing expenditures data should reveal to management the extent to which progress is being made in either installing the new technology, putting the pieces of a new program into place, or bringing a new product or service to fruition. An innovation for which little is being spent may be considered to be inactive, which may indicate problems that management should investigate further.

If a project approach is taken to managing an innovation, regardless of its type, then collecting such data is easier because the project is simply given an account number to which all expenses are charged. In six of the seven high technology companies studied, such an approach was taken. In four of these seven firms, individual researchers always filled out sheets to account for their time. And in five of the seven firms, individual researchers filled out requisition slips for all purchases, which they did at least some of the time in the other two firms. Thus, management was able to exert a fairly tight degree of control in these companies.

The importance of accurately recording cost information about projects is highlighted by the U.S. government, which requires it of defense contractors. When it was discovered that General Dynamics had inaccurately attributed costs to some projects, the company became temporarily ineligible for further government contracts.[13]

Conventional wisdom has it that tightly controlled employees are not as likely to innovate than their less-controlled counterparts (unless, of course, one considers the innovativeness required to beat the system). It seems incongruous, then, that the seven high technology divisions serving as the source of examples here should so tightly control their research scientists and engineers. These companies depend heavily upon innovation for survival, and, in fact, three of them could be considered highly innovative.

Further analysis of the way in which budgeting was done in these companies, however, indicates that there may be ways in which tightness of control in some aspects of budgeting can be neutralized or balanced by relatively loose control in its other aspects. One method of reducing the possible resistance of employees to tight budgetary control is to involve them in the initial stages of the budget-setting process. In three of the seven companies, individual researchers were at least sometimes influential in determining their own budgets. In one pharmaceuticals firm, for instance, when budgets were being prepared, scientists and their supervisors were asked to fill out a sheet with their anticipated needs; then they negotiated the amounts with the group manager, who was two levels below corporate vice president of R&D.

R&D managers or directors are often in a better negotiating position with general management if they can prove their function's credibility by demonstrating how their budget requests contribute to the accomplishment of the organization's overall plans and long-term objectives. In fact, general managers may want to request this kind of information as part of the budgeting process, not only from R&D directors, but from other innovating departments. Another way in which negotiating can be facilitated is for innovating units to develop a scorecard for general management to show how past budgets have been used to innovate in tangible ways that have been particularly valuable to the rest of the organization.[14]

Another method of easing the tension that can be caused by tight budget control is to refrain from feeding back to projects' managers reports of their expenses. In five of the seven companies, monthly project expense reports were never sent to each project's principal investigator, although the next highest level of management often had that data available.

Finally, if individual researchers are not evaluated on the basis of their ability to keep spending within budgeted amounts, then it is less likely that they will feel negatively affected by a tight budgetary system. Although in two of the seven companies, researchers were sometimes evaluated on their ability to control costs, in four of them, they were rarely evaluated on this basis.

What these findings seem to indicate, therefore, is that managers of the innovation process can soften the impact of tight budgetary control on innovators in order to prevent them from becoming inhibited by excessive concern about preventing waste and remaining within budgets. While managers themselves may feel budgetary pressure, they can absorb some of it without passing it on, thereby acting as buffers. Interventions, when necessary because such control indicates that an innovation is in trouble, can be done informallly on a more personal basis.

Organizing Human Resources

As one experienced innovator and company president notes, "Unless the organization is properly designed to carry out innovation, it will fail." Indeed, study after study reveals the importance of organizational design in determining the successful outcome of innovation.[15] While chapter 3 discussed issues relevant to designing a climate for idea generation, the following analysis concentrates on those relevant to implementation.

Based upon accumulated managerial experiences, empirical research, and this author's observations, three ideas warrant consideration when creating structures to mobilize human resources for the final stages of any type of innovation. They are:

1. More structure is needed for implementing ideas than for initiating them.[16]
2. The degree of innovation is a determining factor in the amount of attention that general management should pay to designing special organizational structures to support and control it.
3. Structures should simultaneously protect innovative activities from pressures of routine functioning while maintaining connections to enable it to be easily absorbed by the organization when it is sufficiently developed.[17]

Implementation Requires More Structure than Initiation

Organizations' structure consists of the following dimensions: (1) the extent to which labor is divided into specific, differentiated tasks, (2) the comprehensiveness and specificity of rules and procedures, (3) the number of levels and status differences among the steps in the authority hierarchy, (4) the degree to which decision making is shared by all organizational members, and (5) the degree to which decision making is objective or "impersonal." In general, more structure means specialized division of labor; comprehensive, specific rules and procedures; many levels in the authority hierarchy; and centralized, top-down decision making based upon objective criteria.[18] More structure, then, gives management more control in order to reduce uncertainty and to standardize performance toward achieving organizational goals as the innovation is tested, refined, and put into place.

When creative solutions are sought to organizational problems during the initiation phases of innovation, however, too much structure shuts off the rich, multidirectional flow of information and rapid shifts of thinking that are required. Indeed, structure may be one of the problems to be solved. For instance, when Du Pont decided to return to its strategy of improving earnings growth with technological breakthroughs, its management had to eliminate some of the many layers of the company's hierarchy, which was characterized by marked status differences. The number of strategic planning meetings, necessary signatures, and long reports was also reduced.[19]

Instead of formal mechanisms for getting new ideas, general managers must rely primarily upon informal, interpersonal relationships among individuals and groups throughout the organization. These links are the less visible, more emotional and value-driven "infrastructure"[20] or culture[21] needed to produce "inventions" that have the best chance of becoming "innovations," that is, successfully used.

Relying upon this informal system to actually put an innovation in place, given inevitable resistances, however, almost guarantees that it will take longer and cost more than anticipated. There is too much opportunity for conflict among individuals and groups that can catch the innovation and kill it in the cross fire. Shifting to reliance upon formal structures, then, protects the innovation from the organization's "immune system" that mobilizes to reject foreign intrusions.

One effective way to make the shift from informal to formal structures is to make the innovation the responsibility of one individual who insures that it goes through proper procedures and meets organizational standards or that changes in procedures and standards are made to accommodate the new thing.[22] That is, credible, powerful people are needed to fit new products, administrative systems, and production processes into the organization.

These people may have such formal titles as project or product manager. They may also be known as "champions," "godfathers," or "sponsors." A growing body of literature describes in detail what kind of people they are and what kinds of things they do to get their innovations accepted throughout the organization.[23]

In pharmaceuticals company F, those who put themselves on the line to implement innovations were called "lightning rods." The role became formalized when a highly profitable antiulcer drug finally made it through the tightly controlled product evaluation system after it had almost been killed.

The idea for the new drug came in 1963, and by the late 1960s, management tried to reject it. There was no marketing pull for it because it was the first such product in its class. Only R&D was pushing for its launch, despite low sales forecasts of $18 million a year. Within the R&D department, however, an "outspoken, articulate, zealous, aggressive" man stepped forward. He knew the business very well, and by the end of the 1970s he managed to get the product introduced to the market.

In addition to a project manager and/or a "champion," the weight of top management's authority is needed to shape the expectations of the rest of the organization and to insure the discipline needed to keep costs down and meet deadlines regardless of forces to the contrary. In some innovative companies, general management "blesses" approved projects in symbolic ways in order to convey to the rest of the organization their legitimacy and importance.[24]

Among the formal structures more commonly used specifically for innovation are written procedures for testing and finalizing new products[25] or new technological processes or programs to be adopted. Oversight committees or review boards may also be established to monitor innovations' progress toward completion. It is not unusual for such groups to require a schedule of progress reports and budget evaluations. Finally, innovations may be turned over to entirely new units whose sole responsibility is to bring them to fruition. Such units may be project teams, committees, departments, or affiliated but separate companies.

The Degree of Innovation Determines the Need for Special Units

As discussed in chapter 7, because of their nature as systems, organizations are disrupted more by revolutionary innovations than by evolutionary new things. One reason for the varying degrees of disruption of the organization's routine functioning is that radical innovation usually requires knowledge, skills, and/or experience that incumbent employees may not yet have. Thus, new people may need to be brought in, or incumbents may become distracted from routine tasks as they learn what is needed. Compared to incremental innovations, radical innovations also make more new and different demands for time, space, people, and money on units that did not initiate them.

Because of its tendency to be disruptive, combined with its perceived high risk and deferred rewards, radical innovation generally needs special treatment by general management. That is, general management should be aware that not only does radical innovation need to be protected from the rest of the organization, but the organization needs to be protected from the innovation process. Therefore, it is likely that a special new grouping of people will need to be associated with implementing radical innovations.

Not surprisingly, such innovation in the organization itself to accommodate whatever the radical innovation is adds to the complexity of the process. It heightens the likelihood that the organizational implementation issues of power over and competition for resources will cause resistance problems. Because any time a new organizational accommodation is made, it can very well compound the difficulties that the innovation itself may undergo, it is possible to "over-organize" for innovation. That is, creating special groups or appointing special individuals to oversee the implementation process when it may be that none are needed (as in the case of evolutionary innovation) can cause unnecessary problems. Therefore, general managers should think carefully about whether and how to use special units.

Whether a new organization is to be temporary or permanent should also be carefully considered by its designers. Three approaches may be taken to formally organizing to test and finalize any kind of innovation: (1) using permanent, existing structures without forming any special groups, (2) establishing temporary new project teams to work within existing structures, and (3) designing temporary or permanent new units such as entire offices, departments, or divisions.

If speed and flexibility are essential in implementing the innovation, if the project is not of gigantic proportions, if the implementers have other pressing responsibilities to which they must return, and/or if the implementation is to be a concentrated, but relatively brief effort, then it appears sensible to use temporary groupings of personnel. Such conditions are often, but not always, characteristic of more evolutionary innovation.[26]

On the other hand, for innovations that may need a more gradual, slower implementation period, as is often true of more radically new things, a permanent unit can provide continuity and stability over several years' time. Furthermore, permanent special innovation units (such as Alcan's "design and demonstration organization") can attract personnel well-versed in solving problems particular to new things. The top-level support and funding that is essential in creating such units also signals the organization's commitment to significant innovation, even if it takes a long time to come to fruition.[27]

Structure Should Simultaneously Differentiate and Integrate Innovation

Separate special units for innovating, especially venture groups, have been difficult to use successfully. Among the reasons cited for their failure are: top management turnover; shifts in corporate strategy or financial condition; top management's expectation of positive results in five years or less; corporate level enforcement of annual budgets; use of large staffs of planners, analysts, and consultants; and forcing venture managers to trade off among conflicting political and corporate objectives.[28]

Many of these problems imply that despite their nominal separateness or differentiation from the routine operations of the rest of the organization, in the unsuccessful cases, venture units were not quite protected enough from budgetary and political pressures. Instead of reducing bureaucracy, in some instances, it was increased with staff personnel. The whole point of a venture unit, however, is to provide innovation with the kind of nurturant, long-term–oriented environment that the rest of a large, mature bureaucracy simply cannot provide.

Nonetheless, it is possible to isolate venture units too much or set them up with such special privileges that they become the target of resentful, envious forces within the organization which try to undermine their effectiveness. Among the lessons that one former Exxon executive learned from that company's failure to use the venture concept effectively was that personnel in such units should expect to be integrated back into the rest of the organization. Furthermore, he learned that bountiful corporate financing can be too much of a good thing because it reduces the venture unit's entrepreneurial drive.[29]

Striking a balance between differentiating and integrating organizational structures for innovation, therefore, appears to be important in effective design.[30] Regardless of the type of structure used (permanent existing, temporary project, or separate units), unless innovation is protected enough to evolve while also connected enough to be fitted back into the ongoing organization, it is likely to be hampered or to fail.

The concept of simultaneous structural differentiation and integration is now widely accepted in the field of organization theory. It has been used to understand the differences in the ways that different functional departments operate in order to successfully adapt to the key elements in their respective environments.[31] What is proposed here is an adaptation of this concept. Innovation can be a very different task from most of the others that organizations perform. It appears that there is no one best way to organize human resources to carry it out.

It is worth considering that an innovation's degree of newness is related to the degree of differentiation and integration required in organizational structures to execute it successfully. The more radical the innovation, the more separate and special its structure must be, yet the more important it is for general management to insure that bridges are there to bring it back into the organizational mainstream when it is ready. Conversely, incremental innovations require fewer special structures and correspondingly less management attention to reintegrating them into the organization's routine.

An adaptation of the contingency model of organizational design to the task of innovation, that is, fitting structure to the type of innovation being executed, should help to minimize organizational implementation problems.

Notes

1. Dale L. Flesher, Tonya K. Flesher, and Gerald U. Skelly, *The New-Product Decision* (New York: National Association of Accountants, 1984), p. 140.

2. Ibid.

3. Jay Galbraith, "Designing the Innovating Organization," *Organizational Dynamics* (Winter 1982), pp. 5–25.

4. Rosabeth Moss Kanter, "Supporting Innovation and Venture Development in Established Companies," *Journal of Business Venturing*, 1 (1985), pp. 47–60.

5. Rosabeth Moss Kanter, *The Change Masters: Innovation for Productivity in the American Corporation* (New York: Simon and Schuster, 1983).

6. Kanter, "Supporting Innovation."

7. Louis R. Pondy and Jacob G. Birnberg, "An Experimental Study of the Allocation of Financial Resources within Small, Hierarchical Task Groups," in Michael Schiff and Arie Y. Lewin (eds.), *Behavioral Aspects of Accounting* (Englewood Cliffs, N.J.: Prentice-Hall, 1974), p. 236.

8. For a discussion of the pros and cons of participation in budgeting, see Selwyn W. Becker and David Green, Jr., "Budgeting and Employee Behavior," in William J. Bruns, Jr., and Don T. DeCoster (eds.), *Accounting and Its Behavioral Implications* (New York: McGraw-Hill, 1969), pp. 327–41; and Edward E. Lawler, III, and John Grant Rhode, *Information and Control in Organizations* (Santa Monica, Calif.: Goodyear, 1976), chapters 5–6.

9. Flesher et al. *New-Product Decision*, pp. 121–22.

10. Michael Schiff and Arie Y. Lewin, "Where Traditional Budgeting Fails," in Schiff and Lewin, *Behavioral Aspects*, p. 132.

11. Kanter, "Supporting Innovation."

12. Kenneth A. Merchant, *Control in Business Organizations* (Boston: Pitman, 1985), p. 79.

13. John Koten and Tim Carrington, "For General Dynamics, Scandal over Billing Hasn't Hurt Business," *Wall Street Journal*, April 29, 1986, pp. 1, 20.

14. Michael F. Wolff, "Negotiating Your R&D Budget," *Research Management* (May-June 1985), pp. 8–9.

15. *New Products Management for the 1980s* (New York: Booz Allen & Hamilton, 1982); and Stanley Baran, Peter Zandan, and John H. Vanston, "How Effectively Are We Managing Innovation?" *Research Management*, (January-February 1986), pp. 23–25.

16. Gerald Zaltman, Robert Duncan, and Jonny Holbeck, *Innovations and Organizations* (New York: John Wiley & Sons, 1973); and Frederick A. Johne, "How Experienced Product Innovators Organize," *Journal of Product Innovation Management*, 4 (1984), pp. 210–23.

17. Galbraith, "Designing;" and Kanter, "Supporting Innovation."

18. Zaltman et al., *Innovations*, p. 132.

19. Alix M. Freedman, "DuPont Trims Costs, Bureaucracy to Bolster Competitive Position," *Wall Street Journal*, September 25, 1985, pp. 1, 19.

20. Johne, "Experienced Product Innovators."

21. Kanter, "Supporting Innovation."

22. Dorothy Leonard-Barton and William A. Kraus, "Implementing New Technology," *Harvard Business Review*, No. 6 (November-December 1985), pp. 102–10.

23. Modesto A. Maidique, "Entrepreneurs, Champions, and Technological Innovation," *Sloan Management Review*, Vol. 21, No. 2 (Winter 1980), pp. 59–76; Thomas J. Peters and Robert H. Waterman, Jr., "Corporate Chariots of Fire," *Across the Board*, (May 1983), pp.40–47; and Kanter, *Change Masters*.

24. Kanter, *Change Masters*; and Gian F. Frontini and Peter R. Richardson, "Design and Demonstration: The Key to Industrial Innovation," *Sloan Management Review*, Vol. 25, No. 4 (Summer 1984), pp. 39–49.

25. Johne, "Experienced Product Innovators."

26. Hirotaka Takeuchi and Ikujiro Nonaka, "The New New Product Development Game," *Harvard Business Review*, Vol. 64, No. 1 (January-February 1986), pp. 137–46.

27. Frontini and Richardson, "Design and Demonstration."

28. Norman D. Fast, "Pitfalls of Corporate Venturing," *Research Management* (March 1981), p. 21.

29. Hollister B. Sykes, "Lessons from a New Ventures Program," *Harvard Business Review,* Vol. 64, No. 3 (May-June 1986), pp. 69–74.

30. Ibid.

31. Paul R. Lawrence and Jay W. Lorsch, *Organization and Environment* (Homewood, Ill.: Richard D. Irwin, 1969); and James D. Thompson, *Organizations in Action* (New York: McGraw-Hill, 1967).

9
Testing and Finalizing

General management has a four-part role in the last phases of the innovation process. One part is to decide upon the extent and general nature of the testing to be done. The others are to evaluate the results, to determine whether or not to finalize innovations, and to participate in formally "launching" those that successfully pass the tests. While the project leaders or other implementation managers who are directly responsible for the new thing need enough technical knowledge about it to procure specialized services (such as market research or pilot production), general managers need to be aware of two important nontechnical issues as they make their decisions.

One issue is the need to test new things at all. Is this part of the innovation process always necessary? It is important for general management to diagnose the need to test a given innovation because such testing incurs a variety of costs. In order to make a good decision about how to proceed through the later phases of the innovation process, therefore, these costs must be weighed against the benefits of testing.

Traditionally, the new-product/service innovation literature has not questioned the assumption that testing always must be done in order to minimize the risk of expensive market failures. Much has been written about market testing these forms of innovation. Less work, however, has been done on the need to test new production processes and administrative forms and procedures. Indeed, it appears that the underlying problem of the need to test as applied to all forms of innovation has not yet been studied formally.

Another general management concern is the nature and quality of the testing itself. That is, general managers should be able to ask good questions to insure that whatever testing is performed will in fact achieve the purposes for which it is done in the first place. In general, valid testing follows the scientific method for conducting experiments. Managerial control is needed to avoid wasting time and money on invalid tests that do not contribute to effectively making the ultimate decision about whether or not to finalize the innovation.

The Benefits and Costs of Testing Innovation

The primary purpose of testing any kind of new thing is to get information about it to decide whether it is worth having. This phase of innovation is a more focussed, formal, specialized version of the earlier reality-testing phase. It differs from feasibility-testing, however, in that the question to be answered is no longer "Can this new thing be done?" but, rather, "Should this new thing be done?"

Once having committed itself to investing resources to formally test an innovation, management's goal should be to determine whether its ultimate users want it, and in what form they will find it most acceptable. If users want the new thing in a form that the organization can provide, then it should be finalized. Thus, the main benefit of testing innovation is that management can learn more about the likelihood of its ultimate success, that is, acceptance by users.

In order for this learning to occur, both the organization and the users must themselves learn enough about the new thing to generate the data that management seeks. Testing the innovation permits both the organization and users to actually experience the new thing, resulting in more accurate reactions to it. In fact, in some instances, actual experience with an innovation may be the only way to reveal technical problems such as design flaws; unavailability of personnel, materials, and supplies; and inability of existing facilities to accommodate the innovation.

Additionally, experience can provide better information about hidden business problems such as unacceptable dollar costs, violation of safety regulations or other laws, and prohibitively long time periods required to use or produce the new thing. Users may not know the extent to which the new thing is a genuine improvement over what currently exists or is available from competitors until they have had a chance to experience it for themselves, often over an extended period of time.

While testing has its costs, it can provide this valuable experience without requiring the often significantly greater investment needed to put the innovation into effect on a large scale. If well done, then, testing can save money over the long term.

General Electric's experience of developing a completely automated nuclear fuel reprocessing plant during the 1970s is a case in point. Although the plant's major components had been tested, and the project continued to have a favorable economic prognosis, a pilot plant was not built. When the large-scale plant was constructed and tested using nonradioactive materials, such severe technical problems arose that the entire plant was ultimately abandoned and written off as a loss.[1]

There are three types of costs that testing innovation incurs: monetary, competitive, and organizational. Monetary costs are those required to put the innovation into testable form, whether this means building a prototype and producing a limited number of new items, purchasing services on a trial basis, or printing drafts of administrative forms. Financial resources may also be used to design and administer specific tests, as is done by market research specialists for new products and services or by organizational development specialists for administrative innovations.

Competitive costs take two forms, both of which may be difficult to quantify. One form is the cost of leaking information to competitors about the innovation, thereby enabling them either to rapidly copy it (with improvements) or to prepare some other way to thwart its success. Market testing is particularly vulnerable to this type of cost. Competitors can and do pose as users or customers, obtain the innovation, and then take it apart and use whatever information they can get to copy it.[2]

Another form of competitive cost incurred by testing innovation is the delay that can be caused by

1. The length of time needed to perform enough valid tests,
2. Tests that are flawed and must be redone, or
3. Problems identified by the tests that must be solved before the innovation can be finalized.

If the organization is trying to gain an advantage by beating its competitors to the market or in adopting a new technology, then delays can thwart this goal.

Like competitive costs, organizational costs are also difficult to quantify. They are incurred when testing the innovation leaks information to those within the organization who oppose it and want to prevent it from being put into place. It is conceivable that resisters will learn enough about the new thing to develop arguments against completing it or to erect barriers to it that are impossible to overcome.

Of course, the competitive and organizational costs of testing innovation are not always incurred, and they are difficult to anticipate with any certainty. In most instances, therefore, general managers are likely to give most consideration to monetary costs when weighing the pros and cons of entering this phase of the innovation process.

A Scientific Approach to Testing Innovation

Testing innovation is analogous to testing anything else in that an attempt is made to discover the innovation's effect upon users, the organization, and the environment. In order for tests to be valid so that they are worth the time, money, and effort expended to conduct them, they should meet a number of basic requirements.

To get good information about what the new thing does and how it is received, the tests themselves must be valid, that is, they must measure the properties they are intended to get data about and they themselves must not introduce distortions in the data obtained. Experts specializing in testing methods and procedures, therefore, should be used. "Quick and dirty" testing may cause more problems than it solves.

One requirement for validity is that the innovation should be in "finished" form. Of course, the very purpose of the test is to permit it to be better tailored to users and the organization, but the new thing should be as close as possible to the form in which it was originally intended and promised in the proposal that top management agreed to support. Whatever changes in the innovation, if any, are made as it is prepared for testing should be accurately and fully noted. In this way, management can track the nature of the innovation as it evolves, thereby facilitating interpretation of later test results.

Another requirement of valid testing is that the conditions under which the tests are done must duplicate as exactly as possible the conditions in which the innovation will ultimately exist and be used. There are two major sets of conditions: those associated with the source that provides the innovation and those associated with its users. "Source conditions" include availability and quality of personnel, space, supplies, and equipment needed for the innovation to occur. "User conditions" are the targeted audience's needs, attitudes, demographic characteristics (such as socioeconomic status, age, and education), skill and knowledge levels, and potential demand for the new thing.

In reality, it is almost impossible to exactly duplicate all the necessary conditions in testing an innovation. Furthermore, it may be prohibitively expensive to do so, although the costs should be put into perspective. The better the test, the more valid the data, the better the decision that management can make. At any rate, managers should require that discrepancies between test conditions and anticipated real conditions are noted. Once again, doing so will permit a better understanding of the reasons for the test results that will be used in reevaluating and finally deciding about the innovation.

Test results should be viewed and used with a degree of caution that matches their limitations, which is the main reason for knowing what these shortcomings are. Even the most valid tests, however, cannot make managers' decisions for them.[3] This point is obvious when one considers that if several tests are done, it is quite common for the innovation to look very good according to some results, but less good according to others. In some instances, management must use judgment to decide how much more investment, if any, can be made in modifying the innovation, in what ways it should be modified, and how much time should be allowed to do so.

Whether or not more testing should be done after the changes are made must also be determined by management because of the additional expense incurred. If the testing is to be repeated, the same requirements apply. Not only has the innovation changed in ways that must be noted, but also the source and user conditions may have changed. These differences should be noted. The more dynamic the innovation's organization, industry, and other environment, the more important it is to identify these changes, all of which take resources to track thoroughly.

Types of Innovation Tests

Using a scientific approach to testing innovations does not necessarily mean that the tests are strictly quantitative and statistical. In fact, for radically new things, there is insufficient data available to make such testing feasible.[4] A variety of tests exist, including prototype creation, semiworks or pilot-plant production, cooperative customer testing, market evaluation, test marketing, trade shows, and demonstrations.[5] Many of them were developed originally for new products, but, with some tailoring, they could be used for any kind of innovation, including new administrative procedures or programs.

All of these tests provide information either about the organization's ability to attain the innovation (that is, about the innovation's source) or about the user's response to the innovation. Thus, there are two main types of tests: "source tests" and "user tests." It is traditional for source tests to precede user tests because the new thing must be made tangible in sufficient quantity and quality before it can be introduced to a sample of users. Nonetheless, it is possible for feedback loops from users to providers to be so short that both kinds of testing occur almost simultaneously.

Source Tests

In developing new-product innovations, the phase that either immediately precedes or follows economic analysis and selection is commonly called the prototype phase. It consists of three subphases: model building, bench-scale production, and pilot-scale production. Each subphase represents the making of a successively larger quantity of the new thing for test marketing. Not all of the subphases are necessary for every innovation, however, and some guidelines can be used to determine which, if any, should be undergone.[6]

All kinds of innovation do, in fact, go though a prototype phase even though a physical model may not be made and nothing must be manufactured for testing. For example, in generating a new service, the advertising copy must be written, physical facilities such as an office and telephones must be procured, and personnel must be trained in order to make the service available to a sample of clients. The essence of the prototype phase is that the innovation is prepared for testing.

The main function of the phase is to test the organization's (the source's) ability to make it available for either internal or external use. In order to try out a new technology, the adopting organization must be able to get demonstration models or samples to use. Furthermore, the relevant department must be able to use them. That is, it must make space available and have sufficient electrical power, computer capacity, or trained personnel.

The Preparation Phase and Its Subphases. In taking an integrative approach to innovation, therefore, it is more appropriate to call the prototype phase the "preparation" phase. Like the prototype phase, the preparation phase has subphases, "sample" and "trial run." They are fewer in number and more broadly defined than those pertaining to new-product development. The first subphase can be called the sample subphase because one or a few copies of the new thing are made available for trial use, but normal operations are not called upon to get involved in either making or using it. The sample subphase, then, corresponds to the model-building and bench-scale production subphases of new-product development.

The sample subphase serves to transform an idea into a tangible, usable item. It provides information about the design of the new thing and the relative difficulty of following any specifications that may be written. Additionally, the organizational unit that must make it tangible and functional is tested on its skill and willingness to do so as originally envisioned.

The sample subphase of creating a new research institute in a college, for instance, consisted of writing a detailed description of the institute's objectives, structure, and functioning. It included a fairly specific organizational chart, a description (including qualifications) for the executive director's position, and a flowchart for teaching and research funding proposals and recommendations. The sample subphase of a new automated inventory system would be the purchase of a demonstration disk and its installation on the organization's existing computer.

If there is to be more than one set of prospective users of something new, several replicas of the sample may need to be available. The sample subphase reduces uncertainty about whether or not it is possible and economical, in terms of both time and money, to have or to make more than one unit of the innovation. One of the main delays in the commercialization of laser technology, for instance, was just this problem of reproducibility.[7] This subphase begins, then, to generate more accurate manufacturing or operating cost information.

Also, if design flaws or mistakes in meeting specifications are going to be made, it is usually less expensive and time-consuming to spot them during small-scale operations. For example, Rolls-Royce went into bankruptcy due to losses sustained when it tried to sell a jet engine having defective carbon filament compressor blades for which a prototype had not been created and tested.[8]

In the trial run phase the organization's normal production or operating systems are used to either make enough copies of the new thing to test or to use the new thing in a limited way under realistic conditions. It corresponds to the pilot-scale production phase of new-product development. An example is the conversion of one branch of a multibranch bank into a test site for a new check-cashing procedure. Normal operations are prepared, although on a limited basis, to test the innovation by training the tellers and printing signs and brochures for customers.

This subphase, then, provides an opportunity for problems in the production process itself to surface. Can the new equipment adjust to the material it must process? Can the necessary pressures, precision, and tolerances be achieved? Is the staff familiar with and skilled in the procedures required? Also, experimentation may be done to evolve the most economically efficient process.[9] By facing these problems while the innovation is still in its preparation phase, management may be able to modify the original sample. In many cases, it is much less expensive to adjust a sample or prototype than it is to adjust manufacturing equipment or an entire process.

Whenever something new is done for the first time, mistakes are inevitable. During the trial run subphase, the operating system (including both people and equipment) is able to adjust to working with the innovation without the degree or pressure from other departments that may be felt once it is completely implemented. During this subphase, the operating system should become proficient enough with the new thing to respond fairly easily to demands that will be made on it in the future by other departments in the organization.[10]

In new-product development, it is during this subphase that the manufacturing function of the company becomes most important. If formal pilot facilities are not available, normal production schedules may have to be interrupted to accommodate a new-product run. Any problems caused by the new product may wreak havoc in what may be an otherwise smoothly running, routine operation. The same may be true of other kinds of innovations requiring the services of the computer information systems, human resource management, or accounting departments. The way in which the relevant function reacts to new products at this phase should indicate to top management how innovative, flexible, and skillful it is.[11]

Decision Criteria for Entering the Subphases. There are four basic criteria that are useful in deciding which, if any, of the subphases of preparation an innovation should undergo. They are: (1) the innovation's degree of newness, (2) the existence of a sample used during the reality-testing phase, (3) the expected size or scope of operations once the innovation is completely implemented, and (4) the expected cost of operating to make or to use the innovation.

If the new thing is highly innovative, management should not have spent much energy in gathering facts and figures about it during the feasibility assessment phase because relatively little solid data are available. By this time in the life of the innovation, however, more data should be available, and even more will be generated as the idea is made tangible. Therefore, the preparation phase is essential for radically new things, but may be a waste of resources for incrementally new things.

If several copies of a sample of the innovation have already been created for use in the feasibility assessment phase, then the sample subphase of preparation should be skipped. If test results indicate the need for reworking the innovation in some way, however, then the phase may need to be repeated. If what was proposed during the selling phase was described in very general terms, with details to be worked out later, then the preparation phase is when they should be hammered out.

It does not make sense to enter the trial run subphase of preparation if the innovation will never be made or used on a large scale. If it is to be made or used on a small scale, the innovation's originators, the company's engineers, or the suppliers' customer service representatives should expect to work closely with users to solve problems that arise once the innovation is put into place.

The trial run subphase can be useful for mass-produced items or large-scale operations because any manufacturing or operating errors made during this phase will be made on a more contained scale. Thus, waste and the costs associated with it should be minimized. Also, the accelerated learning needed to rapidly reduce unit costs and, thus, ensure economies of scale is best achieved during the trial run phase.

Keeping in mind that another purpose of this phase is to minimize costly start-up mistakes, if the new thing is very inexpensive to make or to use in the first place, it should not be as necessary to learn on a small scale how to make it or use it. This is particularly important if, for instance, the new product has a very short life cycle and it is critical to get it onto the market as quickly as possible. Thus, the trial run subphase may be skipped.

At the other extreme, an innovation may have a very high initial usage cost because it requires a large investment in new manufacturing equipment or conversion to a whole new technology. In such a case, it does not make economic sense to prepare a sample and a few copies of it for testing before deciding whether or not to continue with conversion to the new technology.

Alternatives to actual model creation, which include computer simulation, may need to be investigated. For example, semiconductor company B never makes prototypes of its semiconductors. Instead, the engineers look at existing products. All new ideas for semiconductors are tested by computer simulation. Then, an initial product is built. This "initial product" may cost $100,000 to actually produce.

In summary, if the cost of an innovation during the preparation phase is expected to be either extremely low or extremely high, then small-scale production or operations may be neither necessary nor economically sensible, especially if costs diminish greatly in a large-scale production or operations, as they normally do. Small-scale operations should be used when costs are moderately high no matter what the scale is or when large-scale operations are expected to increase unit costs.

By using these four criteria, management should be able to determine ahead of time which of the subphases of preparation an innovation needs. However, with four criteria, each of which has degrees of applicability, every innovation represents a unique combination, and making the decision can be a complicated task. There are no hard and fast rules. Judgment is always required.[12] Table 9–1 presents one way through the maze.

User-Tests

As with the other testing phases of innovation, when something new is ready for user-testing, management's first consideration should be whether or not it wants the new thing to go through this phase. A number of criteria are available to help in making the decision. The same logic applies for this kind of test as for deciding whether or not to undergo the preparation phase. In simplified terms, user-tests' purposes are: (1) to increase knowledge, thereby reducing uncertainty and (2) to save money *in the long run* by preventing costly innovation failures. To the extent that user-testing promises to achieve both these goals, it should be employed.

Table 9–1
Criteria for Entering the Preparation Phase

	Preparation Subphases	
Criteria	Sample	Trial Run
1. Innovation		
High	yes	yes
Moderate	yes	yes
Low	no	no
2. Existence of model		
Complete	no	yes
Incomplete	yes	yes
None	yes	yes
3. Scale of operations		
Small	yes	no
Large	yes	yes
4. Operating cost		
Very high on small scale; lower on large scale	no	no
Very high on both small and large scales	yes	yes
Moderate on small scale; higher on large scale	yes	yes
Moderate on both scales	yes	yes
Moderate on small scale; lower on large scale	yes	no
Very low on small scale; higher on large scale	yes	yes
Very low on both large and small scales	yes	no

Before management even begins to decide whether or not it wants to user-test an innovation, however, it needs to make sure that this major step is feasible. Positive answers to the following questions indicate that testing can be done:

1. Can the company afford to test users?
2. Can the innovation be available in sufficient quality and quantity by the time that we expect to begin testing?
3. Are our existing personnel competent and reliable enough to carry out whatever responsibilities they have in conducting the tests?

If user-testing is generally feasible in the organization, then management should consider the specifics of each innovation as it approaches this phase.

Decision Criteria for Applying User-Tests. Two sets of criteria are available. The first set is the nature of the goal to be achieved by user-testing. Some criteria in this category will help management to decide if the test will increase its knowledge; other criteria will help to decide if the test will save money. The second category is the nature of what is being tested. A few criteria in this category are related to the innovation itself, while most criteria are related to the context in which the innovation would be tested. Table 9–2 presents the criteria grouped into these categories.

As was true for its previous decisions about whether or not to test something

Table 9–2
Criteria for User-Testing

Nature of Subject Being Tested	Nature of Goal Achieved	
	Knowledge	Savings
Innovation itself	Degree of newness	Cost of getting enough to test
	High = yes Moderate = maybe Low = no	High = no Moderate = maybe Low = yes
Users	Availability of other data sources about correctness of assumptions about users	Cost of large-scale introduction
	Yes = no No = yes	High = yes Moderate = maybe Low = no
	Availability of other data sources about users' knowledge of and attitude toward the innovation	Expected usage level when innovation is established
	Yes = no No = yes	High = yes Moderate = maybe Low = no

new, management begins by assessing the candidate's degree of innovation. If it is highly innovative, then management can conclude that, yes, according to this criterion, at least, it should test users. The more innovative a new thing, the less knowledge is available about it, and the greater the uncertainty about its likelihood of success on a large scale. User-testing's purpose is served. Furthermore, not only does the company have little knowledge about it, but the company's competitors should also have little knowledge about it. Therefore, management can assume that it will take the competition longer to develop either a directly competing item of their own or a strategy that will hinder the new thing's competitive advantage.

If management assesses the innovation to be moderately innovative, then other criteria must be considered before deciding whether or not to user-test. If the innovation is merely an improvement of what exists or is very similar to something already established, then sufficient information should be available about it already. The purpose of testing is not being served.

Furthermore, the company's competitors are more likely to be able to initiate a similar innovation or modify their marketing strategy with enough speed to seriously invalidate any information that such a test could provide. For these reasons, if the product's degree of innovation is deemed to be low, table 9–2 indicates that no, the company should not user-test that particular innovation.

One large personal care products company, for instance, rarely does actual test marketing unless a product is patentable. Most of its new products are "idea products" that are easily stolen or preempted once they are introduced on a small scale. Whether a market test is done by this division or not depends upon the degree of risk of the product's failure. If it is low, no testing is done. The fact that the cosmetics and toiletries business does not require high capital investment helps to reduce the stakes in new-product introduction. However, all products are subjected to medical tests, and high standards have been set. Such tests cost between $30,000 and $150,000.

The next criterion for user-testing is availability of information from other sources. For example, management's experience with similar innovations, published reports, or outside experts hired as consultants may provide the necessary information without exposing the innovation to competitors. Additionally, companies whose product or service innovation takes the form of introducing lower-priced versions of what already exists on the market may rely upon retailers' information about sales volume or upon salespeoples' reports of the most popular available items. Trade shows are another substitute for formal test marketing. The innovation can be introduced to merchandisers or dealers whose reactions are used as a surrogate for customers' reactions.

The general principal involved in this part of the decision is that if management already has enough information about users or if it can get high quality data elsewhere with the same or less cost and effort, then it probably should not test market.

At the bottom of the "Knowledge" column in table 9–2, the number of "yes"s, "maybe"s, and "no"s should indicate whether or not, on this set of criteria at least, formal testing should be done. Moving to the "Savings" column, the same process can be repeated. If the cost of producing enough of the innovation to permit a test is high, then not very much will be saved by testing. Certain innovations require such a large capital investment for pilot plants and/or new equipment and facilities to produce even the smallest quantity that the cost is prohibitive. For instance, new products in such industries as automobiles, steel, chemicals, and semiconductors often are not test-marketed for this reason.

If, on the other hand, introducing the innovation on a large scale is expected to be very costly in terms of advertising, promotion, and new administrative and sales force salaries and expenses, then user-testing should be done. Similarly, the larger the scale of the introduction or the higher the level of usage that is possible, then the more sense it makes to user-test because more could be lost if users do not accept the new thing.

Making the Final Test Decision. To finally decide whether or not to user-test the innovation being considered, sum the "yes," "no," and "maybe" answers from both columns in table 9–2. The decision should be based on the set of answers with the highest sum. If the "maybe" set is the highest, then the assessments of the innovation's newness and costs should be reevaluated. Upon what are the judgments that it is "moderate" based? Are the judgments confirmed by other managers familiar with the type of innovation and the users?

If after this reassessment, "maybe" answers still predominate, use the other two sets to decide. If there are more "yes" answers than "no," for example, then user-test. Alternatively, formal decision analysis may be used. In new-product development, this technique permits managers to break the test-marketing decision into a series of sequential "subdecisions," each of which is based on the possible outcomes, including total investment and risk preference or "utility." Probabilities are assigned to each outcome, based on management's best judgment.[13]

Management should remember, however, that test market and other user-test results are projections or predictions about the innovation's performance on a large scale. For market tests done for new products, these projections are done statistically, based on the small sample that was actually tested. The projections are only as sound and reliable as the design of the test, the accuracy of the measures, and the statistical model used to analyze the data.

Controlling the Testing Phase

The knowledge and technology necessary for improving forecasting are growing constantly. High-quality market research is expensive enough to consider as an investment in its own right. Given the difficulty of obtaining sound predictions, however, management should not economize at this phase of innovation if it decides to undergo it. Therefore, general managers and innovators should be careful, highly selective consumers of market research or other kinds of user-testing services. Even if these services are provided within the organization, managers should comparison shop and check references.

One reason that some companies do not test users is that their innovators are convinced that users are not qualified along the proper dimensions to provide good information. This belief is especially prevalent among specialists in high technology companies. In their view, users are not sophisticated enough to understand the new thing, and have nothing against which to compare it if it is radically new. A variation on this attitude occurred in one silver and giftware company, in which designers wanted to lead consumers' taste in design. They believed that, in general, users did not have good taste and could not be trusted to provide data that these designers were willing to use.

In fact, in any kind of enterprise having a strong artistic or intellectual component (such as architecture or publishing), a tension between business and aesthetic or moral values is inevitable. This conflict may surface around the question of how much an innovation should be tested with users. It is up to general management to resolve this issue; the way in which it does so reflects its own value orientation.

While user-testing is not always necessary, managers should make the decision based upon the premise that the primary purpose of user-testing is to gauge user acceptance. If the new thing is assumed to be too sophisticated, too avant garde, or too difficult to use, then verifying that notion provides critical information. It can help managers to gauge whether or not education can make the innovation acceptable to users. Data about how much and what kind of education is needed can also come out of such testing. Simply assuming away the need to test because users are not qualified can be very dangerous and should not be the sole criterion used to decide on whether or not to engage in this part of the innovation process.

Another testing issue over which general management needs to exert control is that of where in the organization an administrative or technological innovation will be demonstrated. Some implementation managers who want their innovation to succeed so that their careers will be enhanced may choose a demonstration site that will not provide valid data. Selecting the most innovative or sophisticated users as a sample may make the new thing look good to top management. If prospective users in the rest of the organization view this sample as very different from themselves, however, they may not find this demonstration to be convincing. General management should scrutinize plans to user-test something new by demonstration to insure that the testing site is representative of ultimate users, rather than one that produces the politically desired effect.[14]

Finalization

If the user test is conducted and completed as planned, a great deal of information should be available for general managers to use. It should indicate the accuracy of estimates made in the proposal, such as sales volume, profitability, and cost savings. User-test data can be used to check the correctness of the proposers' assumptions about the innovation. These assumptions and resulting estimates, therefore, should be the benchmark or standard for evaluating the innovation's preintroduction performance. This last major decision is once again economic; therefore, in many ways it repeats the earlier selection phase.

Positive responses to the following questions mean that the innovation has successfully passed the testing phase:

1. Has the innovation reached or surpassed the originally assumed level of acceptance in terms of such considerations as market share and/or capacity utilization?

2. Are the projected volume, profit, or resource savings generated by this acceptance equal to or greater than the original estimates?

3. Are as many users sufficiently aware of the innovation to try it as had been assumed?

4. Are users' attitudes toward and use of the innovation the same as had been originally assumed?

5. Have as many users tried the innovation as was expected? Have as many of these trial users used more of the innovation than was expected?

6. Have competitors reacted to the innovation as was originally expected?

Successful passage of the trial phase nearly always means that the innovation will be completed.

Unfortunately, however, even minimally successful passage of it sometimes means that the innovation is completed regardless of its problems simply because of the resources that have been expended to do the testing. In pharmaceuticals company F, the decision-making committee asks, "Given what we know about the new compound after the early animal and human tests, and given the amount already spent at the development stage, when we've put in 46 percent of the required time and 80 percent of the investment, should we submit a New Drug Application (NDA) to the Food and Drug Administration?" Approximately 15 percent of new drugs are dropped after the initial batch has been made and before the NDA is submitted. Another 5 percent are rejected before market introduction.

The sentiment "We've committed too much to this new thing to stop now," however, actually undermines the whole purpose of testing. It may take a strong management refusal to continue in order to actually stop innovations that do not keep their proposers' earlier promises. General management, therefore, may need to exert the strongest control over innovation that it has yet used at this final decision-making point.

If the new thing is proposed by organizational members at lower hierarchical levels, it is probably easier to veto completion than it is if general management itself has initiated the innovation. The same point is especially true in smaller entrepreneurial companies in which the major stockholder may very well be the founding inventor who continues to generate new ideas, some of which simply do not make business sense, given the present state of the company or its environment. People who want to keep their jobs may not dare to object to the founder's innovation.

In many companies, a top-level committee, which may be the board of directors, makes the final decision. The closer to the top of the hierarchy an innovation is initiated—regardless of what level has had the responsibility of bringing the innovation to fruition—the more necessary it is for the very top of the organization to determine whether or not it will be finalized. Such top-level control is particularly important to exert over two kinds of innovation: (1) that which has a strategic impact on the entire organization and (2) that which has a significant impact on the organization's environment, regardless of whether environment is defined in physical, legal, or social terms.

Reserving the right to approve or reject even fully developed innovations can give boards of directors and other such overseeing committees the clout needed to prevent a very powerful individual from forcing through a potentially destructive innovation. To have real power, however, the committee must have a sufficient number of members who are "outsiders" not otherwise affiliated with the organization, or who are not appointed by the very official that they are trying to control.

One key way in which this round of decision making about innovation differs from the earlier selection process, then, is that more emphasis is likely to be placed upon decision criteria that are external to the organization. This is especially true when the first economic decision is made at middle-management levels, but the final decision is made at the very top of the organization. Additionally, the more outsiders there are on the highest-level committee, the more probable it is that such criteria as legal ramifications, long-term social effects, organizational image in the industry or sector, impact on the relevant technology's state of the art, or international competitive advantage will be heavily weighted in the final decision.[15] The next chapter considers some of the larger, environmental issues relevant to general managers of organizational innovation.

To put into operation or into the marketplace something new that has passed the trial phase of the innovation process requires the accomplishment of specialized, technical tasks that general management may monitor via progress reports and/or budgets, but with which it does not become directly involved.[16] When something new is ready to be formally introduced, however, either to the organization itself or to the marketplace, general management can assist in smoothing its way by participating in, if not initiating, some kind of ceremony.

In some firms, general managers take new-product–development team members and their spouses out to dinner or hold a party or other event in their honor.[17] Units that have adopted a new production system or that are performing a job in a new way may celebrate the "maiden voyage" or successful first-time—through completion of a task. Humor and imagination in tailoring the symbolic gesture to the innovation can help to win over those within the organization who are still doubtful that the innovation is a good thing.

With such a ceremony, general management is basically promoting the innovation to the organization. The same selling skills that were used to convince top levels to finalize the new thing should be put into play for this finishing touch as well. Of course, if the innovation is a new product, the marketing and advertising functions design its "launch," which may include an organizational event as well as market promotions.

Not only does ceremony publicly signal general management's support for the innovation, it also makes it difficult to disengage from it. For this reason, it should not occur too early in the innovation process. Additionally, management gives recognition, which can be very satisfying, to those who have made the new idea a reality. Celebration of the beginning of new things is one way to create a climate that values and encourages innovation.[18]

Notes

1. Thomas H. Lee, John C. Fisher, and Timothy S. Yau, "Is Your R&D on Track?" *Harvard Business Review*, Vol. 64, No. 1 (January-February 1986), pp. 34-44.

2. Yoram J. Wind, *Product Policy: Concepts, Methods, and Strategy* (Reading, Mass.: Addison-Wesley, 1982), pp. 404-5.

3. William L. Shanklin and John K. Ryans, Jr., *Marketing High Technology* (Lexington, Mass.: Lexington Books, 1984), pp. 94-95.

4. Ibid., p. 98.

5. Edwin A. Gee and Chaplin Tyler, *Managing Innovation* (New York: John Wiley, 1976); Gian F. Frontini and Peter R. Richardson, "Design and Demonstration: The Key to Industrial Innovation," *Sloan Management Review*, Vol. 25, No. 4 (Summer 1984), pp. 39-49; and Wind, *Product Policy*, chapter 14.

6. The ideas in this section and in tables 9-1 and 9-2 are adapted from or reprinted with permission from my earlier work, *How to Manage The New Product Development Process*, Chapter 5. (copyright 1982 American Management Association, New York. All rights reserved.)

7. Robert A. Myers, "Why the Trip from Laboratory to Marketplace Takes So Long," in *Managing Advancing Technology*, Vol. I, edited by the Staff of *Innovation Magazine* (New York: AMACOM, 1972), pp. 188-201.

8. Lee et al., "Is Your R&D on Track," p. 36.

9. Gee and Tyler, *Managing Innovation*, p. 81.

10. Ibid.

11. Ibid.

12. Ibid.

13. For more in-depth coverage, see Glenn Urban and John L. Hauser, *Design and Marketing of New Products* (Englewood Cliffs, N.J.: Prentice-Hall, 1980).

14. Dorothy Leonard-Barton and William A. Kraus, "Implementing New Technology," *Harvard Business Review*, Vol. 63, No. 6 (November-December 1985), pp. 102–10.

15. Rosabeth Moss Kanter, *The Change Masters: Innovation for Productivity in the American Corporation* (New York: Simon and Schuster, 1983), chapter 10.

16. For excellent coverage of the details of commercialization, see C. Merle Crawford, *New Products Management* (Homewood, Ill.: Richard D. Irwin, 1983), pp. 459–636; Urban and Hauser, *Design and Marketing*; and Nan Langowicz, *An Exploration of Production Problems in the Initial Commercial Manufacture of Products*, unpublished doctoral dissertation (Boston: Harvard University Graduate School of Business Administration, 1986).

17. Hirotaka Takeuchi and Ikujiro Nonaka, "The New New Product Development Game," *Harvard Business Review*, Vol. 64, No. 1 (January- February 1986), pp. 137–46.

18. Thomas J. Peters and Robert H. Waterman, Jr., *In Search of Excellence* (New York: Harper & Row, 1982).

10

Integrating Innovation and the Environment

To more thoroughly understand the innovation process and general management's role in it, an examination of the relationship between an organization's external environment and its innovative activities is necessary.[1] Making better innovation decisions depends upon being able to gather information and to formulate criteria from both inside and outside of the organization.

General managers function to some extent as gatekeepers, opening their organizations up to or closing them off from the influence of external factors such as banks' interest rates on borrowed funds, government regulatory enforcement officers, and consulting firms' trainers.[2] One reason for this mediating function is that representatives of external groups commonly seek out general managers for official transactions. General managers' greater authority enables them to speak for their organizations.

The further up in the hierarchy managers are located, in fact, the more regular contact with a wider scope of the organization's environment they are likely to have. Figure 10-1 illustrates the increasing closeness of progressively higher levels of general management to external organizations.

More specifically, general managers link the innovation process within their organizations to the outside world in several ways. Innovation strategies are often formulated partially in response to external threats (such as new laws prohibiting the use of carcinogenic substances) or to external opportunities (such as consumers' increased demand for pure drinking water).

In addition, general managers stimulate lower-level employees to come up with new ideas by bringing back and disseminating problems, information, and resources from their dealings with external groups.[3] Visits to customers and participation in training seminars, industry association meetings, or congressional hearings can spark concerns or enthusiasm in general managers, which they then pass on to others in their organizations.

When general managers require that innovators test their new ideas' feasibility with prospective suppliers or relevant regulatory agencies, they are also integrating innovation with the external environment. Using innovations' an-

SOCIETY

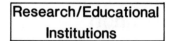

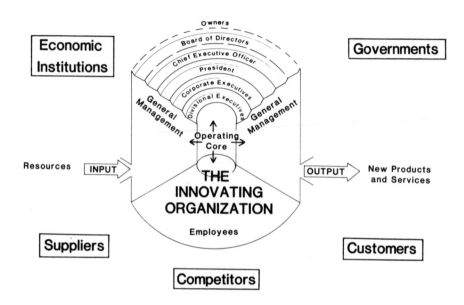

Source: Adapted from R. Edward Freeman, *Strategic Management: A Stakeholder Approach* (Boston: Pitman, 1984), p. 25.

Figure 10–1. The Innovating Organization and Its Environment

ticipated impact on such external groups as customers, competitors, or the community surrounding the company's facilities as criteria to select the best ones to implement is another integrative mechanism.

Finally, when top management publicly announces its company's innovations and provides information about them in press releases, annual reports, or legal testimony, for example, it is acting as a communication conduit to the outside world. Table 10–1 summarizes these five key points of general management involvement in the innovation process, at which innovation and the environment are integrated.

Table 10–1
General Management Interventions Linking Innovation
with the External Environment

1. Formulating innovation strategies. How much, when, and what kinds of new things do we want to do in response to external events?

2. Stimulating new-idea generation.

3. Requiring early external testing of new ideas' feasibility.

4. Selecting innovations to implement based upon criteria that include their consequences for the environment.

5. Introducing completed innovations to the external world and disseminating information about them.

The Environment for Innovation: A General Definition

In the broadest terms, the environment for an organization's innovative activities is the same as that for any other kind of activity. That is, the environment is comprised of a variety of organizations that are not legally attached to it.[4] Figure 10–1 provides a sample of the most common kinds of organizations that affect or are affected by innovations.

It should be noted that a mutually interactive relationship can be conceptualized as existing not only between each of the boxed sets, but also between each set and any or all of the others in the environment surrounding a particular organization.[5] For visual clarity, the web of double-headed arrows that would have blackened the page was omitted, although it belongs in the diagram.

Starting with a company's industry (or set of industries for diversified firms), competitors, consumers, and suppliers all play a major part in the innovation's feasibility, never mind its ultimate success. The relatively recent adoption of the "just-in-time" (JIT) inventory control technique by large U.S. manufacturers illustrates the interconnectedness of organizational innovation and its environment. As its name suggests, this method calls for raw materials and other supplies to arrive at the plant only as they are needed for the relevant part of the production process. JIT's main benefit is that it greatly reduces, if not eliminates, the costs of carrying inventory.

JIT was brought to the United States from Japan by such diverse firms as Harley-Davidson and Xerox. Their Japanese competitors were winning away customers with lower prices and comparable or higher quality. One reason for their competitors' success was the use of the JIT technique, which sparked the U.S. companies' interest in it.[6] Thus, not only was a process innovation adopted as a response to an external competitive threat, but the idea for the response itself also had external origins.

In order for JIT to be implemented successfully, however, the adopting companies' suppliers have to cooperate. They must be willing and able to deliver precisely what has been ordered at precisely the correct time, with no mistakes because there is no back-up inventory or slack. Errors or delays by suppliers stop the innovating firms' production process. Suppliers are typically unaccustomed to doing business in this fashion.

The first U.S. firms to adopt this innovation found that suppliers were reluctant to bear the additional costs of holding inventory themselves and refused to go along. Suppliers, then, were being forced to innovate in some of their operations in order to keep their customers and many were resisting. Firms such as Harley-Davidson, Xerox, and Hewlett-Packard eventually had to innovate beyond the JIT system itself by establishing training programs for their suppliers and by including them in the design phases of new product development.[7]

The adoption of JIT has also created an opportunity for firms in the freight industry to innovate by providing new precision delivery services. Skyway Systems, Inc. is one company that specializes in shipping parts and materials by truck or air to high technology firms such as Apple Computer. Rather than considering components suppliers as its customers as is traditional, however, Skyway's customers are those manufacturers who have adopted JIT.[8]

Economic institutions are another type of external organization, but one that is not necessarily in a company's immediate industry or industries. This set includes banking, accounting, investment, venture capital, and insurance firms. Their rates, charges, and premiums reflect in part the larger society's general economic climate. They supply resources to innovating organization which can, in turn, create demand for new services that provide opportunities for them to innovate.

As the computer software industry emerged in the early 1980s, for example, some of the small start-up companies that developed new programs were financed by venture capital firms.[9] The software entrepreneurs, in turn, needed help in developing business plans and designing administrative systems to run their companies. Thus, some accounting firms innovated by providing new consulting services to small businesses.[10]

The link between research and educational, economic, and innovating organizations is also illustrated by the software industry. It is relatively common for software entrepreneurs to hold Ph.D.'s.[11] In some instances, they originate and develop their programs while working for a college or university. The educational institutions provide these innovators with a relatively regular source of income from their research and/or teaching jobs while they start their small businesses. In turn, the entrepreneurs may hire students as employees, providing them with income and practical experience in their young companies. Universities and colleges also provide accounting and venture capital companies with business courses and faculty consultants who can then be used to provide services for software entrepreneurs.

Domestic and international governments, ranging from city councils to regional and federal bodies and judicial systems, form another set of environmental forces that can be connected to an organization's innovation. In terms of whether this set has a positive or negative effect on innovative activities, however, no generalizations can be made. For example, the uncertainty surrounding the creation and enforcement of tax laws and health, safety, and market regulations has been found to both stimulate and to stifle innovation.[12] It is not even clear whether or not governments' procurement and loan programs, often intended to foster innovation, always do. Nonetheless, many academic and industrial analysts view companies' environment primarily in terms of government organizations.[13]

Defining the Environment in Specific Terms

The way in which any particular organization's general management defines its environment will in large part be based upon powerful individuals' beliefs about the kind of relationship that their company should have with the outside world. One way of conceptualizing these beliefs is to answer the question, "To whom does management think itself to be most responsible?"

Traditionally, managers viewed themselves as being responsible first and foremost to their firms' owners. That is, they saw their primary task as maximizing profitability. The negative consequences for the firm's environment of doing so could be explained away with the assumption that business is a separate, purely economic aspect of society. As long as business generates profits, society benefits at least indirectly, and that is all that business should be expected to accomplish. This point of view has been labelled the "stockholder" approach to managing the relationship between business and society.[14]

Another perspective is that business organizations are just another part of the social system. They are not separate or special. Because they are so closely related to other kinds of institutions and organizations, simply generating profits is not enough to fulfill their obligations to society. They also have a responsibility to avoid intentionally harming these external groups. This set of beliefs is called the "stakeholder" approach to the business–society relationship. An organization's stakeholders are those external groups or organizations who are directly affected by what the organization does or who directly affect the organization in some way.[15]

The stockholder position leads to a relatively narrow definition of an organization's environment. It is basically restricted to suppliers, competitors, and customers, that is, the organization's industry. On the other hand, the stakeholder position assumes a much broader definition, but one that must be tailored to any given innovating organization. For example, not all governmental regulatory agencies or sources of aid affect the operations of software companies. While software start-ups could be impacted by the Small Business Administration, they may have nothing at all to do with the Food and Drug Administration.

One way of defining a particular firm's external environment, therefore, is to draw a "stakeholder map." Such a map includes the names of all organizations that are touched in any significant way by the firm's innovative activities. Conversely, any outside organizations whose activities can directly benefit or harm the firm as it innovates should also be part of the map. All private citizens' watchdog groups, labor unions, investment bankers, insurers, competitors, suppliers, relevant government organizations, and so on could be grouped into sets as in figure 10–1, with the specific relationships spelled out for each.[16]

To go a step further, a list of potential "shocks" from each of these outside organizations to the firm's innovation activities could be drawn up. The probabilities of their occurrence could then be estimated in order to anticipate the extent to which particular innovation projects will be affected.[17]

The purpose of making a stakeholder map for an innovating organization is to provide general managers with a comprehensive view of the environment as a source of new ideas, useful information, funding, personnel, and potential barriers to implementation. Such a map can also be a natural source of decision-making criteria to apply to particular new things at each phase of their innovation process.

Managerial Attitudes That Shape the Innovation-Environment Link

As boundary-spanners between their organizations and the external environment, general managers naturally act as filters. Perceptions of what the environment is like are often based upon assumptions about what is *should* be like and how their organization *should* be related to it. These perceptions naturally limit and/or distort the environment's impact.[18] For example, tax reform can be viewed as a threat or an opportunity; the way in which a firm responds to this external event depends to some degree upon top management's attitude toward it.

Innovation is one important form of organizational responsiveness to its external environment. To analyze past innovation decisions or to make more informed future ones, a model of corporate social responsiveness exists that can be adapted and applied to the specific case of general managers' management of innovation. The Buono-Nichols model identifies four types of responsiveness, based upon two dimensions.[19]

One dimension is whether or not the most powerful top managers, who ultimately determine the firm's direction, have a stockholder or stakeholder view of the relationship of business to society, as was just discussed. The other dimension is whether or not top management is predominantly motivated by self-interest (instrumental rationality) or by a sense of moral duty transcending concern about possible negative consequences for itself when responding to environmental groups (value rationality).

As table 10–2 shows, the interplay of these dimensions results in four types of attitudes toward, or responses to, environmental forces. To use Buono and Nichols's terms, they are productivism, philanthropy, ethical idealism, and progressivism. The sample innovations and kind of criteria used for making decisions about innovation reflect the general type of managerial attitude.

Productivistic Innovation

General managers who believe that their actions are ethical and proper as long as they benefit their firms' owners and do no intentional harm to others are motivated by self-interest. The underlying assumption is that what is good for the self (company) is also good for others (society), and that hurting others intentionally will in all likelihood attract reprisal of some sort. Therefore, one should avoid acting in such a way as to directly harm another.

Actions that benefit firms' owners and managers but have negative consequences for external groups, however, are often difficult to avoid. The concept of "the greatest good for the greatest number" then becomes a guiding principle.

For example, although a new pesticide may damage the ability of some species of birds to reproduce, managers operating on the basis of self-interest would

Table 10–2
The Buono-Nichols Model Used for Managing Innovation as a Form of Corporate Social Responsiveness

Top Management Motive	Assumed Reference Group	
	Stockholder	Stakeholder
Self-interest	Productivism (office automation)	Progressivism (child care services)
	Economic criteria only	Balance of economic and noneconomic criteria
Moral duty	Philanthropy (new drug for a rare disease)	Ethical Idealism (inclusion of employees on board of directors)
	Primarily economic, some noneconomic criteria	Social criteria only

Source: Adapted from Anthony F. Buono and Larry Nichols, *Corporate Policy, Values and Social Responsibility* (New York: Praeger, 1985), p. 74.

weight more heavily the interests of the large number of people who consume the food made possible by the pesticide and the people who will be employed to make it than the interests of the smaller number of conservationists who work to preserve nature.

Managers with a productivist attitude toward the relationship between their organization's innovation and its external environment would define the environment narrowly as the relevant industry or industries. Innovation's ultimate purpose would be to maximize profit and minimize losses. Its more immediate goal would be to enhance the firm's competitiveness. Therefore, only those new undertakings that would not threaten smooth quarterly earnings growth with high investment levels or long time horizons would probably be considered.

Adopting the latest computer and telecommunications technologies to automate a company's administrative offices is one kind of innovation that can result from managers' productivist attitude. Office automation can be viewed as a way of responding to the decreasing supply and increasing educational attainment and salaries of office workers; to the demands of customers and suppliers for more rapid, accurate processing of orders and payments; to competitors' ability to provide better service at lower costs; and to the very availability of affordable technical equipment and know-how that is adapted to the particular industry.[20]

Although the innovating company benefits from the new technology because costs are reduced, productivity increases, and the company is more competitive, the labor market may be harmed by loss of skilled, white collar jobs. Furthermore, workers may be exposed to unhealthful levels of stress, eye strain, and radiation from computer video display terminals.[21] Nonetheless, because profitability is enhanced through cost reduction—managers' most important goal—the innovation is implemented.

A productivist approach to integrating an organization's innovation and environment calls for purely economic criteria to be used at the five decision points listed in table 10–1. In formulating an innovation strategy, management has to decide whether and when the firm is financially able to purchase new computer and telephone equipment. Next, to spark ideas for office automation, management must decide how to define the company's need for it in economic terms. For example, managers could emphasize that overhead costs must be reduced and that it is seeking new ideas for doing so with automation.

When new ideas are generated, management would decide upon limits on how much could be spent. This decision would enable lower-level innovators to contact vendors to test the feasibility of adopting their equipment and services at the prices that the company can afford. In selecting which type of automation system to adopt, general management would be primarily interested in the savings promised and the impact they would have on the environment. The environment would be defined as owners (with impact on profitability), competitors (with impact on ability to win market share away from them), and customers (with impact on ability to increase sales by lowering prices due to productivity gains). The only criteria applied, then, might be initial purchase price and implementation costs including training, lost productivity, and service. In announcing this innovation to its environment, general managers would decide how to restrict the information they disseminate to the savings and greater efficiency that office automation provides.

Philanthropic Innovation

Managers who believe that some of their actions must be taken for their own sake, because they are inherently good, are motivated by a sense of moral duty. Unlike their utilitarian counterparts, they assume that not every action has to achieve a more ultimate goal, such as self-interest. In fact, they are willing to take action even if it will harm them or cost them something because they think it is so important. Thus, managers who highly value advancement of knowledge, helping disadvantaged members of society, or preservation of natural beauty, for example, may feel obligated to innovate in ways that will live up to these values.

Managers with a philanthropic attitude toward the relationship between their organization's innovation and its external environment would, like productivist managers, define the environment narrowly as the relevant industry. Also, they view their primary responsibility to be maximizing profitability and minimizing losses for their company's owners. Therefore, innovations would be undertaken to fulfill a sense of moral duty without detracting from the firm's profitability. Hence, only a limited amount of innovation, within tightly circumscribed economic boundaries, would be considered.

Developing and making available a new drug for the treatment of a rare disease could be a philanthropic innovation. The president of the laboratory at pharmaceuticals company D indicated that his company feels a sense of obligation to use its skills in finding and testing new compounds in order to help consumers who suffer from unusual ailments. No company could ever benefit from commercializing such products because the market is very small and, ideally, could be eliminated with either prevention or proper treatment. Yet, to discover, develop, test, and get U.S. Food and Drug Administration approval for any prescription drug, regardless of the size of its market, costs a minimum of several million dollars and may take up to ten years to complete. Company D carries out its duty by carefully selecting a very few such drugs to develop if the company's scientists discover them. It spends no money to promote or advertise these drugs.

Company D's top management also values higher education and the advancement of knowledge for its own sake. Thus, it provides a limited number of fellowships to externally affiliated scholars and researchers for study in disciplines related to the pharmaceuticals industry. Although the results of this pure research rarely benefit the company directly, its management is willing to support such innovation because it believes that it is inherently good.

The decision criteria used by managers having a philanthropic attitude as they integrate their company's innovation and environment include more noneconomic factors than those used by productivist managers. Yet, economic considerations are still extremely important. For example, in formulating innovation strategy, philanthropic general managers could ask themselves a series of questions, starting with, "What are the problems in our industry that we strongly believe should be addressed?" Next, they could ask themselves, "Could we help by doing something new on a limited basis that would not detract from our profitability? Which problems should we address, with what level of effort, and when?"

In introducing to internal innovators an externally based problem or need, general managers must decide how to present or define it and how much information to give about why the firm has decided to undertaken it. While management is seeking new ideas for development, it wants to limit the amount of effort that people put into generating them. Thus, without making this serious initiative appear like empty rhetoric or a public relations event, management does need to convey what priority it is placing on new ideas. At the reality-testing phase, managers should ask, "Given that we will never make money by doing this new thing, how much are we willing to spend and how long are we willing to spend it?" By making these decisions and conveying them to innovators, they establish parameters within which an innovation's feasibility can be tested.

The most important criteria for evaluating and choosing philanthropic innovations are related to their costs: whether they are within the preestablished limits and the organization's ability to afford to implement them. Nonetheless, managers might add to the more traditional selection criteria that of the extent to which undertaking the innovation in a limited way will really make a difference. Will the new thing be significant enough to satisfy a sense of moral duty? Another noneconomic criterion is whether or not another external group would be harmed in some way by the innovation under scrutiny. In announcing philanthrophic innovations to the public, managers should decide what they are trying to accomplish by doing so as a way of determining how widely and with what media such information should be disseminated.

Ethical Idealistic Innovation

Managers whose attitudes lead them to innovate in an ethical idealistic way are not only motivated by a sense of moral duty. They also believe that their primary responsibility is to society rather than to their firms' owners. Their strongly held values and stakeholder view of the relationship between business and society are generally associated with their belief that radical change is needed in business's role and function.

A basic assumption is that corporations should serve all of society, not just their owners. Business should be a way of bettering human existence, not vice versa. Therefore, the decision criteria are not economic, but rather social, political, or religious. Doing new things for their own sake regardless of the costs to the organization would be quite acceptable to ethical idealistic general managers.

An example of an ethical idealistic innovation is when a firm's top management begins to include nonmanagerial employees on its board of directors. In so doing, employees as representatives of the wider society, with interests that often directly conflict with those of the firm's owners, are given more power to set direction and make decisions than they have ever had previously. Another example would be a firm's establishment of a committee to review its involvements with South African businesses. To pressure that nation to dismantle its apartheid system, the firm would innovate with a new organizational structure, such as a committee, for deciding upon the best way to disengage itself from any relationships with the South African economy.

In both examples, apart from general management's satisfaction in knowing that it had lived up to its values, the most benefit that the innovating firm could expect to derive from these activities is a reputation as a socially responsible organization. In some critics' view, however, such actions might be seen as irresponsible because they drained profits away from society in some way.

Decision criteria to be used in managing such innovations would, for the most part, be different from the ones presented in this book because they are not economic. Such criteria as savings, return on investment, and increased efficiency or productivity are irrelevant unless not achieving any of them would jeopardize the innovation's viability. Decisions about ethical idealistic innovations are based on the dictates of the values and morals of the most powerful people in the firm. Nevertheless, one criterion could be whether or not the new thing is actually accomplishing what it was intended to accomplish without causing worse problems than the one it was meant to solve.

Progressive Innovation

Like ethical idealistic managers, progressive managers of innovation believe that they are as responsible to external societal organizations as they are to their companies' owners. They assume that business can and should be a force for societal change that will improve human existence. Like productivist managers, however, they believe that business's role in social evolution should be limited to those activities that will achieve clear-cut goals, among them the furthering of their companies' best interest.

Progressive innovation, then, anticipates and responds to major trends in the needs and preferences of its stakeholders, including employees, consumers, competitors, and the government. The motivation for doing so is that it is "good for business" to be socially responsible. The actual innovations undertaken are limited to those that will benefit the organization directly, although not necessarily by improving profit levels.

Firms that installed new equipment to minimize or eliminate the toxic effects upon the physical environment of their waste before government regulation made it mandatory are managed progressively. Their voluntary action anticipated a societal trend and may have saved them the expense of lawsuits or having to comply with new regulations under pressure. In fact, such innovation can enable companies to set industry standards and to guide the creation of government regulation. In some instances, such self-regulation makes external regulation—with its accompanying uncertainty, bureaucratic complications, and costs—unnecessary.

One example of progressive innovation is the child-care services offered by some large companies. Making these services available to employees and/or to members of the surrounding community responds to the needs of the increased number of women in the labor force, many of whom have young children. In order to attract and keep talented female employees and to increase their productivity, some firms have begun to modify their benefits packages to include either reimbursement for child care or referral and clearinghouse services to find such care. During the 1970s, a few firms, such as Stride Rite and Control Data, went so far as to establish on-site day-care centers which were also open to non-employee families from the inner-city neighborhoods where the sites were located.

This example indicates that the kind of innovation progressive managers choose in formulating their strategies is not necessarily related directly to their industry and does not need to contribute to profitability in a direct way. Two decision criteria applied during the strategy formulation phase, however, are the extent to which there is a real need for the innovation and the extent to which the company's best interests, broadly defined, will be served at least partially by the innovation.

Again, as with productivist and philanthropic innovation, managers would preset limits on the amount and kind of resources they can allocate to the innovation to insure that their organization does not suffer as a result of undertaking it. If, after investigation, it appears that it is feasible to do the new thing within these limits, then it can be proposed for implementation. Selection criteria would consist not only of costs, but also of the new thing's expected impact upon both the organization and its environment.

In fact, progressive management of innovation implies that any new thing's effects upon the environment, apart from the company's industry, are to be scrutinized carefully and weighed heavily at the selection phase. Although an innovation's negative impact on the firm's environment might not be considered a strong enough reason to stop its implementation, management can at least start the process of finding ways to mitigate the negative outcomes.

Thus, returning to the office automation example, if implementing computerized filing and data retrieval means that file clerks will be deprived of jobs, then progressive managers might include a new retraining program for the benefit of potentially displaced employees as part of the automation project. Productivist managers would not view such a step as their responsibility, and, since its costs could not be adequately justified, they would probably not even consider such a program.

These examples of four different approaches for managing the relationship between innovation and the environment are meant to convey the idea that there is probably no correlation between the type and degree of innovation and the approach used to manage it. That is, a radically new organizational form (such as the "network company"[22]) is as likely to be adopted by a productivist management as by an ethical idealist management. Additionally, the generation of new products and adoption of new organizational procedures could both occur using an ethical idealist approach.

Nonetheless, general managers' attitudes toward their organizations' relationship to their external environments are likely to be an important factor in setting an internal climate for innovation. These attitudes and perceptions pervade decision making at all phases of the innovation process.

Better decisions about innovation can result, in part, from decision makers' heightened awareness of their own underlying assumptions, values, and motivations with respect to this important organizational function. Such self-knowledge can free them from decision-making patterns that yield less than satisfying results. It often takes innovation to innovate! The key to better innovation is better decisions made about it. The more general managers can integrate the wide variety of disparate forces that make up the innovation process, the more effective their decisions about it will be.

Notes

1. Andrew H. Van de Ven, "Central Problems in the Management of Innovation," *Management Science*, Vol. 32, No. 5 (May 1986), pp. 590–607.

2. E.J. Miller and A.K. Rice, *Systems of Organization: The Control of Task and Sentient Boundaries* (New York: Tavistock, 1967); and Henry Mintzberg, *The Nature of Managerial Work* (New York: Harper & Row, 1973).

3. Rosabeth Moss Kanter, *The Change Masters: Innovation for Productivity in the American Corporation* (New York: Simon and Schuster, 1983).

4. Ibid., p. 280.

5. William H. Starbuck, "Organizations and Their Environments," in M.D. Dunnette (ed.), *Handbook of Industrial and Organizational Psychology* (Chicago: Rand McNally, 1976), pp. 1069–1123.

6. Dexter Hutchins, "Having a Hard Time with Just-In-Time," *Fortune* (June 9, 1986), pp. 64–66.

7. Ibid.

8. "For High-Tech Companies, Skyway is 'Just in Time,' " *Boston Globe*, May 27, 1986, p. 52.

9. Ronald Rosenberg, "Tough Times Ahead for Venture Capitalists," *Boston Globe*, December 9, 1984, p. 27.

10. Lee Berton, "Hunting for Small Game," *Wall Street Journal*, May 19, 1986, p. 25D.

11. Richard D. Teach, Fred A. Tarpley, Jr., and Robert G. Schwartz, "Who Are the Microcomputer Software Entrepreneurs?" *Frontiers of Entrepreneurship Research 1986* (Wellesley, Mass.: Babson College Center for Entrepreneurial Studies, 1986).

12. Alfred A. Marcus, "Policy Uncertainty and Technological Innovation," *Academy of Management Review*, Vol. 6, No. 3 (1981), pp. 443–48; National Science Foundation, *The Process of Technological Innovation: Reviewing the Literature* (Washington, D.C.: Government Printing Office, 1983); and Van de Ven, "Central Problems."

13. For a comprehensive review of this topic, see John D. Aram, *Managing Business and Public Policy: Concepts, Issues and Cases* (Boston: Pitman, 1983); and Rogene A. Buccholz, *Business Environment and Public Policy: Implications for Management and Strategy Formulation*, 2nd ed. (Englewood Cliffs, N.J.: Prentice-Hall, 1986).

14. R. Edward Freeman, *Strategic Management: A Stakeholder Approach* (Boston: Pitman, 1984).

15. The following discussion of the stakeholder approach and stakeholder mapping is based upon the ideas of Freeman, *Strategic Management*, and Marcus, "Policy Uncertainty."

16. Freeman, *Strategic Management*.

17. Thomas H. Lee, John C. Fisher, and Timothy S. Yau, "Is Your R&D on Track?" *Harvard Business Review*, Vol. 64, No. 1 (January–February 1986), pp. 34–44.

18. Kanter, *Change Masters*.

19. The following discussion is based upon the ideas presented in Anthony F. Buono and Larry Nichols, *Corporate Policy, Values and Social Responsibility* (New York: Praeger, 1985), chapter 3.

20. U.S. Congress, Office of Technology Assessment, *Automation of America's Offices*, OTA-CIT–287 (Washington, D.C.: Government Printing Office, December 1985).

21. Ibid., p. 19.

22. John W. Wilson and Judith H. Dobrzynski, "And Now, the Post-Industrial Corporation," *Business Week*, March 3, 1986, pp. 64–71.

Index

About the Author

Judith Brown Kamm has consulted for a variety of organizations, including AT&T, General Electric, and the Smithsonian Institution. Her writing has appeared in *Human Relations* and *Journal of Business Strategy*, as well as in several books. A doctor of business administration from Harvard Business School, she is a professor of management at Bentley College in Waltham, Massachusetts.